# FUTURE

*Connecting Child, Church, and Mission*

# IMPACT

## STUDY GUIDE

# FUTURE
## Connecting Child, Church, and Mission
# IMPACT
## STUDY GUIDE

# Dan Brewster

Releasing children from poverty
Compassion
in Jesus' name

Copyright © 2010 by Dan Brewster and Compassion International
Published by Compassion International
Design and production by The Elevation Group
Cover photos by Chuck Bigger

ISBN 978-0-9841169-2-8
Printed in Canada
10 9 8 7 6 5 4 3 2 1

# CONTENTS

# ABOUT FUTURE IMPACT

The material in this book was originally prepared for the course called "Child, Church, and Mission" taught in the Master of Arts Program in Holistic Child Development at Malaysia Baptist Theological Seminary in Penang, Malaysia. It was designed to help students develop their understanding of the meaning and nature of the relationships between child, church, and mission. From a biblical perspective, it provides an overview of the child, poverty, and holistic child development, and thoughts on the relationships between holistic child development and the ministries of the church.

This material may be used as a course of study in seminaries or Bible colleges. We hope this material will also serve as a resource for training other groups and in other venues— such as training for children's ministry workers, workers with at-risk children (specialized groups), and training conducted by Christian child development networks.

## For more information about the course, please contact:

### Dr. Rosalind Lim-Tan
Director: MBTS HCD Institute
40 A-D, Mk. 17 Batu Ferringhi,
Penang 11100, Malaysia
Email: rosalindlyw@gmail.com
Tel. /Fax: 604-881-2462

### Dan Brewster
Compassion International
Email: dan.brewster@yahoo.com
Tel./Fax: 604-890-1440

# HOW TO USE THIS STUDY GUIDE

This guide is designed to help you make the most of the content of *Future Impact: Connecting Child, Church, and Mission.* The sessions will help you both review and retain important points from each chapter in the book.

Toward that end, each session in the guide will feature several common elements.

**1. Four sections** will comprise each session. Those sections are:

### THE NEED

An introduction explaining how the chapter content helps meet a current need of the reader, the church, or children.

### STUDY

A section that highlights key points of the chapter content, asking the reader to reflect on those points.

A section that asks the reader to develop an application, based on the chapter content, relevant to his/her own life, church, or community context.

A closing that challenges the reader to take reasonable action on one item relevant to the lesson within a week of completing the study guide session.

2. **Sessions** offer a variety of ways for the reader to develop greater insights into the study material. Although the items below may not be present in every session, they are commonly used throughout the guide. These include:

- **Insight** items that bring additional information on session topics.
- **Foundation Truths** are brief exercises that lay a foundation of facts, principles, or both.

- **Reflection Questions** challenge the reader to process the chapter content more thoroughly. Write your responses in the note space following the questions, or get a small journal to record these responses.
- **Children Today** features up-to-date statistics on the state of children in our world.
- **Readings** is a brief list of additional source material that may expand your grasp of each chapter's subject matter.

Please note: This study guide is not designed to be self-contained. The reader will need to read each chapter of *Future Impact* before beginning the related session in the guide.

After you've read the relevant chapter in *Future Impact*, you can expect each study guide session to take about an hour. Of course, time will vary depending upon how much time your schedule allows and how much you interact with the material.

God bless you as you seek to better understand His heart and purpose for the children in your life and for children around the world!

# THE CHILD IN
# BIBLICAL
# PERSPECTIVE

# WHY CHILDREN?

# WHY CHILDREN?

## OBJECTIVE

By the end of this session, readers will be able to identify reasons to focus ministry on children in both developing and developed countries around the world.

## KEY VERSE

Psalm 78:4-7: ". . . [W]e will tell the next generation the praiseworthy deeds of the LORD, his power, and the wonders he has done. He decreed statutes for Jacob and established the law in Israel, which he commanded our forefathers to teach their children, so the next generation would know them, even the children yet to be born, and they in turn would tell their children. Then they would put their trust in God and would not forget his deeds but would keep his commands."

## READ

*Future Impact* introduction and chapter one, "Why Children?" Be sure to note any parts of the chapter, including Scriptures that especially impact you in some way.

 ## THE NEED

Why should anyone focus ministry on children today? You probably noted a number of great reasons why as you read through the "Why Children?" chapter in *Future Impact.*

The Church today may not be looking for the children and youth, but they wouldn't have to look far to find them. Children are not a remote or obscure people group. They are found everywhere:[1]

- In all countries, in all socio-economic categories and among people of all cultures.
- In all communities: in its families, its schools, its markets, its playgrounds . . .
- In areas not easily accessible to the gospel.
- In marginalized subcultures: children with special needs, in prisons . . .
- In at-risk situations where circumstances increase the likelihood that they will not have the opportunity to hear the gospel.
- In difficult circumstances associated with religion: children who have been harmed or neglected by those representing the Christian faith.

If nothing else, the Church needs to notice that children surround us—and that most of those children are at some kind of risk.

## Children Today

As noted in chapter one, the risks and ravages facing children are many and complex. Some are as obvious as simply not getting enough to eat. Perhaps 30 percent of the children under the age of 5 around the world suffer from severe or moderate malnutrition. And even in the richest countries, many children are raised in families who live below the poverty line. In spite of vaccines and other measures that protect children in the industrialized world against diseases, millions of children still die each year from diseases that could and should have been prevented.

Despite a near-universal consensus on the life-affirming importance of education, 72 million primary-aged children in developing world have no access to or don't attend school. If those children who ought to be in school held hands and formed a very long line, it would stretch more than twice around the world. Fifty-seven percent of those who should be in school but are not are young girls.[2] Half a million mothers die every year while giving birth leaving babies at extreme risks. Africa has the highest maternal deaths at 51 percent and Asia at 43 percent.[3]

Moreover, in the last decade perhaps two million children have been killed and more than six million children have been injured or disabled in armed conflicts. Tens of thousands of children have been maimed by landmines and thousands have suffered in the upsurge of conflicts fueled by the hunger for land and gems and oil.[4]

## Reflection Questions

1. Think about some of the children and young people you know. Are they "at risk" or not? If so, list a few of the kinds of risks they face.

2. Do you usually notice the children around you or not? What do you think causes you to notice them or not? Think about some ways you might be more attentive to them, especially to encourage and affirm them.

3. Would you characterize your interactions with children as mostly positive, mostly negative, or mostly neutral? Explain.

One major point to take from this chapter in *Future Impact* is the truth that, whether children come from poor or well-off families, virtually all of them are at risk. Consider this material along with what you've read already.

## Children at Risk from Poverty

In many parts of the world, and especially in developing countries, children are at great risk from poverty. Families are seeing increases in the costs of basic food, along with cuts in subsidies for food, health care and education. Many developing countries are finding that children are among the most vulnerable when local economies are opened up to global market forces without investing in and providing adequate safeguards for the poor.[5]

- **Street Children** live in vulnerable situations. We find them sleeping in the dark corners of cities, on the verandas of shops, and on railway platforms. They survive by begging or scavenging. We see them on the roads when the traffic is blocked, as they approach begging, or selling candies or other small items. Poverty, negligence, and broken families lead them to the city streets.
- **Abusive Child Labor** is a serious worldwide problem because of the often irreparable damage it does to

the child. Abusive child labor affects the intellectual development of the child, and unsafe and unhealthy work environments affects their physical and psychological development as well. Moreover, their moral well-being can be seriously compromised when they start working too young. They are more vulnerable to extreme forms of violence and abuse, not to mention the stolen childhoods for those forced to work!

In poor countries child workers are seen engaged in all kinds of work: in brickyards, rubber plantations, paddy fields, fishing boats, garment factories, motor workshops, service stations, and restaurants. They work as domestic helpers in rich people's houses. It is common each morning on the outskirts of many cities and towns to see children rushing behind garbage trucks trying to collect anything that can be recycled among the piles of rotten garbage. Hundreds of children wander the streets offering shoe polishing or selling newspapers, peanuts or fruit, while others beg for money from tourists or foreign aid workers.

- **Trafficking** is a serious threat in many parts of the world. Children are sold for different kinds of exploitation; for sexual exploitation and slavery, for pornography, for forced labor, for war, and even for organ transplantation.

- **Sexual exploitation of children**, including child prostitution, child pornography and trafficking, has always been a serious problem, and more so in a

new era of globalization. Pedophiles and sex tourists cause great damage to innocent children. Surely these are among those causing the little ones to stumble and for whom Jesus recommended the remorseless punishment of having a millstone tied about their necks and being thrown into the deepest part of the sea (Matthew 18:6).

- **Children in, or affected by, war** reflect the changing nature of armed conflict, characterized by a growing percentage of civilian casualties. Every day, more than 20 armed conflicts are being fought around the world, mostly in poor countries. In the past decade alone more than two million children have been killed, and millions more injured or permanently disabled in armed conflicts. Unlike wars in the past, it is now estimated that between 80 and 90 percent of people who die or are injured in conflicts are civilians —mostly children and their mothers.

## Children of Prosperity Put at Risk

It may be difficult to imagine that children of from prosperous families and countries can be "at risk." But as discussed in *Future Impact* chapter one, prosperity can be as great a threat to a child's well-being as is poverty. Some of the "symptoms" of being at risk will differ between children of poverty and children of prosperity. Yet the dangers for such children— and the potential for harm or destruction—is the same.

In whatever culture and situation, for a child, love **is spelled "T-I-M-E!"**[6] Sylvia Hewlett has written an impressive book with the provocative title, *When the Bough Breaks*, which comes from a song often sung by mothers while rocking their babies to sleep:

> Rock-a-bye baby, in the treetop,
> When the wind blows, the cradle will rock.
> When the bough breaks, the cradle will fall,
> And down will come baby, cradle and all.

Hewlett suggests that the "cradle has fallen" for American children today. She says that the main problem is not a resource deficit, but a "time deficit." She details some of the reasons why parents can't spend time with their children:

**No-Fault Divorce**. No-fault/no-responsibility divorce has dramatically decreased the amount of time that parents are able to spend with their children. In the past, American divorce laws were based on the assumption that marriage was a partnership that lasted in most cases "until death do us part." Hewlett notes that prior to 1970 divorce was a legal option but only upon proof of such serious, fault-based conduct as adultery, cruelty, or desertion. Sadly, today, divorce is increasingly seen as "morally neutral, just another option—a life choice no better or worse than staying married."[7] These childish adults don't realize that they cannot leave their spouse and move on to greener pastures without putting the children who are left behind in serious jeopardy.

**More Work, Less Family**. In the past, most mothers especially of young children, stayed at home to care for their children. However, since the 1990s, more than two-thirds of mothers are working outside the home. And while mothers are working more, fathers are also working longer hours. According to one study, the average workweek jumped from 41 hours in 1973 to 47 hours in 1989,[8] and surely it is much more now, 20 years later. Hewlett notes there are Hallmark® greeting cards for over-committed professional parents who find it difficult to actually see their children. "Have a super day at school," says one card, meant to be left under the Cheerios in the morning. "I wish I was here to tuck you in," says another, designed to be placed on a child's pillow at night.[9]

**Adult Values Conflict.** Another major reason why families are in trouble is the shift of values away from the family. All over the world attitudes are changing away from the family. What is happening in America is common in more affluent societies the world over. Hewlett notes that since the late 1960s, adults have been on a quest for personal growth and self-realization:

> Times have changed for both men and women.
> Our new priorities have dramatically diminished
> our enthusiasm for self-denial, delayed gratifi-
> cation, and other less selfish behavior patterns.
> Sacrifice is out of style, and future orientation is
> for the birds. The current getting-giving compact
> reads as follows: I give time, energy, resources to
> a relationship as long as my needs are fulfilled, as
> long as I am stroked. If I become unhappy (or just
> plain bored), I have every right to move on and
> seek what I need elsewhere. The fact of the matter
> is, however, that the qualities needed to succeed in

meeting personal needs often conflict with the qualities needed to succeed as a concerned parent.[10]

**Lacking Money.** There are, of course, those children even in prosperous countries who lack money. Many Africans and Asians whose annual family income is under $1,000 would either laugh or cry at the thought that the middle classes cannot live on $50,000 to $80,000 a year. And yet, ever driven by market economies, parents are spending much more of their energies earning money and not nearly as much on investing time in their children.

**The Myth of "Quality Time."** In their 1987 book, *Quality Parenting*, Linda Albert and Michael Popkin assured moms and dads that by working hard at their interactions with their children, parents could "transform ordinary moments into encounters that, like a healthy diet high in natural foods and vitamins . . . sustains the kids throughout the day," when they had to be busy elsewhere.[11] It's an attractive, idea but it doesn't work.

The main problem with quality time is that there's so little of it! James Dobson compared "quality time" with going to a restaurant when you decide you want to have the best steak in town. Suppose you ordered the most expensive steak on the menu and the waiter returned, plate in hand, and lifted the lid with a flourish. And there was the best steak in town—but only an inch across! No matter how good that steak might be, if that is all we get of it, it simply is not enough. We have to have *quantity* as well as quality. It's the same with quality time with our children.

## Reflection Questions

1. In your opinion, which of the elements putting children of poverty at risk (listed either in *Future Impact* chapter one or this study session) seems to be the greatest threat to them? Explain your response.

2. In your opinion, which of the factors causing well-off children to be at risk (listed either in *Future Impact* chapter one or this study session) seem to be the greatest threat? Explain your response.

3. Which of the at-risk factors listed do you see as potential or real threats to the children in your life? What can you do to limit those risks?

## INSIGHT

### The Bubble Generation

Older youth today who are exposed to a regular diet of electronic and cyberspace communications fall into a that group author Tom Hayes calls "The Bubble Generation." The following characteristics describe them:

- They don't watch a lot of TV or listen to commercial radio.
- They don't tolerate commercials—and they don't have to.
- They are very mobile.
- They rarely use e-mail—it is too slow.
- They are social and private at the same time.
- They reject overly slick, overly produced content and messages.

Do these characteristics describe any of the young people you know?[12]

*Future Impact* chapter one brought out a number of relevant points to answer the question, "Why children?" Review them here:

- Children are the most numerous "people group" on the planet.
- They are also the ones who suffer the most. Millions of children around the world are trapped in poverty, or suffer the ravages of hunger, disease, neglect, exploitation and abuse.
- All children are at risk. Millions suffer from poverty, while millions of others suffer from prosperity.
- It is important to care for children because the childhood years are the formative years—the "clay is still soft."
- Children are made in the image of God, and have an innate "transcendence," which must be protected and nourished.

## Reflection Questions

1. Of the points listed to the left, which one do you feel offers the strongest reason or opportunity for ministry to children? Why?

2. As you see it, what practical action(s) can be taken to respond to this point?

# CALL TO ACTION

The purpose of the call to action in each of these lessons is to help you determine something you can do in response to the material you've encountered.

This week, what action step will you take to make the case for children as a needed focus for mission and ministry? Perhaps you'll decide to take your pastor or missions board chairman out for coffee to discuss the place children have in your missions budget. Maybe you're a pastor and can talk with your church leaders about somehow improving your ministry to children. Or will you talk with a child or young person about ways to avoid being put at risk?

Whatever your response, write it below along with a deadline *within seven days* by when you will take action. (An important note: If your response requires more than a week to enact, it's probably too ambitious. Choose something to do that can be accomplished *this week.*)

# WHAT THE BIBLE SAYS ABOUT CHILDREN

# WHAT THE BIBLE SAYS ABOUT CHILDREN

## OBJECTIVE

Upon completing this lesson, the learner will be able to discuss and apply a wide range of biblical insights on God's heart for children from a variety of Scripture passages.

## KEY VERSE

Matthew 18:6: "But if anyone causes one of these little ones who believe in me to sin, it would be better for him to have a large millstone hung around his neck and to be drowned in the depths of the sea."

## READ

*Future Impact* chapter two, "What the Bible Says About Children." Be sure to note the Scriptures and themes of the chapter that have the highest immediate impact on you.

# THE NEED

People believe many myths about children. One I remember very well is the myth I held about my own children, yet to be born, when I was a single adult. I'd watch married friends with children struggle with their offspring in, say, a grocery store. Their children would get fussy if the shopping took just five minutes too long. My children would never be that way.

Then, of course, my wife, Alice, and I met and married. Over time, I discovered that as advanced as our gene pool might be, our children were just as likely to fuss and throw fits of impatience as any other children—especially in grocery stores. My myth about other people's children was destroyed. (That was probably a good thing.)

In much the same way, many people believe the myth that the Bible has very little to say about children. This chapter and session should destroy that myth and help us better embrace the value and role of children in the Scriptures.

## Reflection Questions

1. How are children (Christians and non-Christians) generally viewed and treated both at home, in school, and in public in your culture? Are they valued and celebrated, or viewed as insignificant or a nuisance?

2. What are some myths you once held about children? How did you discover that your myths about children were flawed?

3. What Bible account of a child means the most to you at this moment? Why?

## INSIGHT

Children are not an afterthought in the Bible: *child*—121 times; *children*—448 times; *son* or *sons*—2,700 times; (not counting the references to Jesus as the Son of God); *firstborn*—100+ times; *boys* and *girls* 196 times. There are also dozens of stories about or including children. All together the child and family-related words occur more than 8,000 times.[1]

This chapter in *Future Impact* featured many Bible passages which, combined, can refine almost anyone's perception of the value and purpose of children.

## Reflection Question

Which three Bible passages referenced in the chapter (either in the body text or the notes) meant the most to you as you reviewed them? How would you use these passages to influence someone's thinking about children?

The chapter features a number of key ideas and themes to consider. Among them are:

- Children are created with dignity.
- God is a defender of the fatherless.
- Children can understand the things of God.
- God uses children for special tasks.

- The Father/child relationship, analogous to God's relationship with us.
- Children being created to praise God and His glory.
- The "already" and "not yet" aspects of both the kingdom and the child.
- The need for "child-likeness" in the surprising teaching that we all must be born again.
- God's expectation that parents will train, teach, love, and respect their children.
- The community is also crucial for nurture of children.

## Reflection Questions

1. Which of the above do you believe would most likely shatter a longstanding myth about children held by people in your church and/or family? What would bring that change of perceptions?

2. What other ideas about children would most likely bring positive change to the way people look at children?

## Foundation Truths: Reading Scripture with the Child in the Midst

*The disciples were arguing amongst themselves about who would be the greatest in his coming kingdom. Jesus, knowing what they were arguing about, responded by taking the child into his arms and said, "Unless you change and become like little children, you will never enter the kingdom of heaven"* (Matthew 18:3).

If we take Jesus seriously, then we must pay attention to this. The child in the midst is often missed!

The child in the midst is the starting point for this course. Many, (perhaps most) readers of Scriptures have overlooked just how prominent children are throughout. For much of the Church today, children have been the "Great Omission!" We have failed to see how much *theology* and Christian *practice* are tied to, illustrated by, or only understood in the light of the *child in the midst.*

Reading *with the child in the midst*, we may see that we may have had our priorities mixed up in the **Church**. We may have underestimated the potential of child ministries and of children as both objects of and agents for **Mission**.

## Reflection Questions

1. Out of the Bible stories you reviewed and others you know, which child character in the Scriptures do you believe (besides Jesus Himself) was most likely to be underestimated by those around him/her? Why?

2. Which child in your life today are you most likely to underestimate? Why?

Sometimes faulty thinking about children, especially in the local church, can frustrate those who want to take practical steps to help children in one's community and around the world. Take the time now to review the insights offered by Dr. Keith White in chapter two before answering the next reflection questions.

## Reflection Questions

1. Having reviewed White's insights in chapter two, which two of them do you think have the most impact on you? Why?

2. How would you explain those insights to bring positive change for children as you discuss them with your local church?

White carefully considers the consequences of the Church's misunderstanding of Scripture and children. As stated in chapter two, White writes, "What if we have misheard or neglected God's revealed teaching about children and childhood? What of the likely effects of such a process on the history and current life and shape of the Church? What if by default we have not been salt and light in God's world? What if our vision of the kingdom of heaven is a pale reflection of what Jesus revealed?[2]"

## Reflection Question

1. As you see it, what are some of the consequences of the Church misunderstanding Scripture and God's heart and purpose for children?

**APPLY IT**

We can bring many positive applications for children today from the timeless principles of the Bible we just reviewed. Sadly, we can also see a terrible pattern of child neglect and exploitation present in Bible times that continues to this day. Review the "Neglected and Exploited" section in chapter two before answering the following reflection questions.

## Reflection Questions

1. Which of the issues in the "Neglected and Exploited" section surprise or anger you the most?
   Explain.

2. What practical action(s) can you take to help bring a solution to this issue?

Consider these grim statistics about children and youth today:

## Children Today[3]

- An estimated one million children enter the commercial sex trade every year.
- More than 91 million children under 5 are growing up with debilitating hunger.
- 134 million children have no access to any school whatsoever.
- 15 million children are orphaned as a result of AIDS.
- 246 million children work, with 171 million engaged in the worst forms of child labor.
- 265 million children have not been immunized against any disease.
- Over one-third of children have to live in dwellings with more than five people per room.
- Over a half billion children have no toilet facilities whatsoever.
- Almost half a billion children lack access to published information of any kind.
- 376 million children have more than a 15-minute walk to water or are using unsafe water sources.

## Reflection Questions

1. Which of the issues in the "Children Today" section surprise or anger you the most? Explain.

2. What practical action(s) can you take to help bring a solution to this issue?

3. Do you believe it would help or hinder you to ask others in your local church or fellowship to join you in bringing a solution to this issue, or the issue you identified in the "Neglected and Exploited" section, at this time? Explain.

4. What are some local issues that hinder children in your community?

5. Which of those local issues do you feel you could help address effectively? Who might you need to help you in your task?

6. What plan of action can you take with your local church to make the biblical issues surrounding children better known? Develop your response with practical details, even though it may take some time to put them into action.

## CALL TO ACTION

Remember, the purpose of the call to action step in each session is to help you determine something you can do in response to the material you've encountered.

This week, what action step will you take to help yourself and others become more aware of what the Bible really says about children? You could read and meditate on several of the verses that include children and begin to read Scripture "with the child in the midst." Perhaps you'll think of one child whom you can, help, encourage, affirm, in your church or neighborhood, or plan how you will share the Bible insights about children from this session with a friend.

Whatever your response, write it below along with a deadline *within seven days* by when you will take action.

## Reading

"What the Bible Says About Children" by Josephine-Joy Wright, *Celebrating Children*, 18-32

"A Little Child Shall Lead Them: Rediscovering Children at the Heart of Mission" by Keith White (plenary paper presented at Cutting Edge conference 2001); find it at http://www.viva.org

# THE MINISTRY OF CHILD DEVELOPMENT

# THE MINISTRY OF CHILD DEVELOPMENT

## OBJECTIVE

**Upon completing this session, the reader will be able to:**

- Show, from a biblical standpoint, that care for the needy is central to the heart of God.
- Provide a definition of holistic child development and state clearly some essential characteristics of what it is and what it is not.
- Understand essential aspects in facilitating holistic development.

## KEY VERSE

Proverbs 30:7-9: "Two things I ask of you, O LORD; do not refuse me before I die: Keep falsehood and lies far from me; give me neither poverty nor riches, but give me only my daily bread. Otherwise, I may have too much and disown you and say, 'Who is the LORD?' Or I may become poor and steal, and so dishonor the name of my God."

## READ

***Future Impact* chapter three,** "The Ministry of Child Development." Along the way, be sure to note any information or insights in the chapter that are important to you.

## THE NEED

There's an old, old tale of a group of blind men who wanted to find out what an elephant "looked" like. In the tale, each man was led to a different part of the elephant and encouraged to learn what he could about the elephant.

The first grabbed the trunk, and immediately the elephant began to make its trunk writhe and wriggle. The blind man could barely hold on. He said to the others, "An elephant is very much like a huge snake. It hates to be held. It is warm and wrinkly."

The second man, who had been led to the elephant's tail, said, "That's curious. I think the elephant is very much like a rope with a brush at one end."

The third man in the group had been led to one of the elephant's legs. He responded, "Not at all. This animal is built like a pillar on a temple—thick and stout and immoveable."

The fourth had been examining one of the elephant's tusks. "I don't find that to be the case. The elephant is smooth like polished wood, rather slender, and coming to a point."

The moral of this story is that *you must see the big picture if you want to truly understand something*. The work of child development is often presented as meeting the physical needs of children. Many focus on the need to clothe and feed children. That's important but not the whole picture—nor is education alone or even spiritual development alone.

To understand child development, we must see its big picture. This session, as it reviews chapter three, will help us do that.

## INSIGHT

In the Old Testament the word *salvation* can be translated wholeness or completeness. It's not just about a salvation decision that puts us in right relationship to God so that we can enjoy heaven forever. It is about a completeness of life that is aligned with the principles of the God's laws, which bring goodness and wholeness into our lives. That goodness and wholeness is not just spiritual. It is physical, economic, and social. It is a goodness and wholeness in every aspect of our lives.

In Deuteronomy 5:9-10, God says, "I, the LORD your God, am a jealous God . . . showing love to a thousand generations of those who love me and keep my commandments." How do we enjoy the full blessings and provisions of God? By aligning ourselves with His laws and instructions. God's laws and instructions have consequences. Verse 16 says, "Honor your father and your mother." Why? so "that you may live long and that it may go well with you." How do you help children and families get to the place where their lives are going well? By helping them to know and follow God's laws. It's one of the principles God has built into the way this world works.

Again, in Deuteronomy 5:29: "Oh, that their hearts would be inclined to fear me and keep all my commands always." Why? "So that it might go well with them and their children forever." And in 5:33, "Walk in all the way that the LORD your God has commanded you, so that you may live and prosper and prolong your days in the land that you will possess." Understanding and following God's instructions for our lives is the foundation for wellness.

## Reflection Questions

1. As you see it, what might be the consequences of a child development strategy based on only a partial understanding of a child's needs?

2. Can you think of an example where a child was helped in one area of life and not others?
   What were the results?

God desires wholeness for each of us, including the poor and oppressed in our world.

Chapter three brought out a number of ideas about the necessity of developing a specific and focused approach to child development. Key themes in this chapter included:

- The Old and New Testament reveal that God has always been concerned for the poor and oppressed.
- There is nothing wrong with wealth by itself. God is against the wealthy only if they oppress the poor, are not willing to share from their abundance, or if they set their hearts on their wealth.
- Holistic child development is a ministry and must include the whole person.
- A healthy self-reliance is an important goal of holistic child development.
- Facilitation of holistic development involves raising awareness, increasing knowledge, skills and attitudes, relationship building, modeling, and resource linking.
- Christian holistic development is a journey that is centered around Bible truths.
- Holistic child development is, therefore, helping the child to become more and more what God wants him or her to be.

## Reflection Questions

1. In your own words, describe some of the characteristics of biblical wholeness.

2. Who in your life is someone who lives out biblical wholeness?

3. What does that person do that helps him achieve such wholeness?

## Reflection Questions

1. Which of the ideas in the checklist on the previous page do you think would most likely help your church's or fellowship's approach to child ministry? Explain.

2. In your opinion, which of the Scripture passages you reviewed in chapter three formed the strongest argument for understanding child development as a holistic process? Why? (You may select more than one passage if you like.)

Chapter three noted the work of John B. Wong in explaining biblical wholeness. Wong says the concept of shalom (peace) in the Old Testament aligns with the idea of Christian Wholism, which I believe to be the basis of Christian holistic child development. "Shalom," he writes, "which occurs some 250 times in the Old Testament,

> Shalom, which occurs some 250 times in the Old Testament, has a basic meaning of completeness, soundness, welfare, peace, contentment, peace with God, making whole, making good, restoring what was lost of stolen (Joel 2:25, Exodus 21:37). The word embodies the meaning of material prosperity in comprehensive meaning of rest, freedom from care, safety, trustfulness, and ease; communal well-being in contrast to war; and a state of law and order leading to prosperity. It denotes bodily health; contentedness on living and at death. It also has the sense of salvation (Isaiah 43:7, Jeremiah 29:11; 14:13). It has a social and political reference beyond the personal dimension. It is associated with righteousness, concrete ideas of law and judgment.[1]

## Reflection Questions

1. In your own words, explain the connection between righteousness, law, shalom, and wholeness.

2. Taking into account the Scriptures and the material in chapter three, what interventions do you think should be a part of a Christian holistic child development initiative?

**APPLY IT**

Future Impact suggests that a key result of Christian holistic development is a greater self-reliance or self sufficiency, trust, dependence, or confidence within themselves.

## Foundation Truths: Seven Characteristics of True Compassion[2]

In Marvin Olasky's important work called *The Tragedy of American Compassion*, he provides a useful discussion of the characteristics of true compassion, (or true development) in a helpful A, B, C sequence:

**Affiliation:** True compassion takes place in the context of the family, church, and community (Genesis 2:18 says that "It is not good for the man to be alone"). The objective of true compassion is to restore natural affiliation with the immediate family, extended family, and mediating institutions—church, organizations, and clubs. Disaffiliation occurs when we hand out food, clothing, or other assistance indiscriminately.

**Bonding:** True compassion requires a personal connection to the individuals (John 1:14 states that "The Word became flesh . . ."). It is demonstrated in knowing their names and "walking in their shoes." (In Compassion International, our sponsorship encourages a kind of bonding between sponsor and child). This significant relationship is important to the sponsor and child.

## Reflection Questions

1. How is self-reliance manifested in your culture? Is self-reliance in childhood or youth perceived positively or negatively?

2. What activities can you think of that develop self-reliance or self-sufficiency in children and youth?

3. What activities can your church host or develop that would promote self-reliance or self-sufficiency in children and youth?

4. How could you encourage self-reliance or self-sufficiency in the children within your sphere of influence?

The well-known James Yen poem says it well: "Go to the people, live among them, learn from them, love them. Start with what they know, build on what they have . . ."

**Categorization:** The Bible discriminated between deserving and undeserving poor:

1. Deserving poor: orphans, elderly, incurably ill, accident victims (Zechariah 7:10; Matthew 19:21).
2. Laboring poor—able and willing to work (2 Thessalonians 3:10).
3. Undeserving poor: intemperate, shiftless, anti-social, criminal (1 Timothy 5:3-8).

Categorization demands the tough love we see in 2 Thessalonians. 3:6-10: " . . . keep away from every brother who is idle. . . . For you yourselves know how you ought to follow our example. We were not idle when we were with you. . . . we gave you this rule: 'If a man will not work, he shall not eat.'"

**Discernment:** Not everyone is deserving of assistance. True compassion sometimes means we have to say "No." Jeremiah 17:9 reminds us that "The heart is deceitful above all things . . . " Well-intentioned and warm-hearted indiscriminate aid breeds dependence and poverty. Compassion without discernment is foolish compassion.

**Empowerment:**[8] True compassion involves empowerment. Empowerment is providing education and job opportunities which will lead to restoration of dignity, self-worth, and independence. Everything we do should have a learning component. To work brings dignity (Genesis 2:15); "I saw that there is nothing better for a man than to enjoy his work. . . ." (Ecclesiastes 3:22). Nothing creates dependency faster than to deny education and work.

**Freedom:** True compassion requires freedom to become what God wants the child to be. Olasky says, "We are a world of 169 countries, and only about 25 of them have made it economically. They were able to do so because the citizens (rather than government) had control of their energy and creativity. It boils down to one word: freedom."[9]

**God:** True compassion nurtures the spirit as well as the body. As we have already seen, True compassion springs from the heart of God. ". . . the LORD, the compassionate and gracious God, slow to anger, abounding in love and faithfulness, maintaining love to thousands, and forgiving wickedness, rebellion and sin" (Exodus 34:6-7). It is said that people and cultures become like the gods they worship. Truly, a world without Christ is a world without compassion.

## Reflection Question

1. List one concrete action that would help a child develop in each of Olasky's areas on the previous pages.

# CALL TO ACTION

This week, what action step will you take to promote Christian holistic child development? Will you suggest the development of a reading or recreation program for youth and children to go along with your church's spiritual development program? Will you remind children in your life that God cares about what happens while they play and study math as well as while they learn Bible lessons?

Whatever your response (and you never need to feel tied to my suggestions), write it below along with a deadline *within seven days* by when you can take action.

## Reading

"God and the Poor" by Ronald Sider, *Rich Christians in an Age of Hunger*, 39-64

*The Tragedy of American Compassion* by Marvin Olasky, 101-115

"Development: Bounded, Centered, or Fuzzy?" by Daniel Brewster and Gordon Mullenix, *Together 50 MARC Publications*, 10-13

*Christian Wholism: Theological and Ethical Implications in the Postmodern World* by John B. Wong

# A SPIRITUAL UNDERSTANDING OF POVERTY

# A SPIRITUAL UNDERSTANDING OF POVERTY

## OBJECTIVE

Upon completing this session, the learner will understand poverty as a *spiritual* problem fundamentally, and where worldview may create tendencies toward wholeness and life or toward destruction and poverty.

## KEY VERSE

John 10:10: "The thief comes only to steal and kill and destroy; I have come that they may have life, and have it to the full" [or "more abundantly" [KJV]].

## READ

***Future Impact* chapter four, "A Spiritual Understanding of Poverty."** Take special note of the material that might help you explain the spiritual nature of poverty, including poverty's causes and the difference a worldview makes.

# THE NEED

What one *thinks* about poverty almost certainly affects how one *deals* with poverty. Anyone doing development work must grapple with questions like, "What are the causes of poverty?" and "Why are children poor?" After all, the point of most development work is to alleviate both the causes and effects of poverty. Jesus tells us "the poor we will always have with us" (Mark 14:7). He also made it clear that we must do what we can to aid them in accordance with Deuteronomy 15:11: "For the poor will never cease to be in the land; therefore I command you, saying, 'You shall freely open your hand to your brother, to your needy and poor in your land.'"

Clearly, Jesus was right. We see the poor all around us. We can see it in the skinny children whose parents cannot feed them, in the boys and girls trafficked into sexual exploitation or sold into bonded labor to pay a parent's debt, and in the eyes of the street children and child beggars at the traffic lights. Even in a world of unprecedented progress and technological innovation, more than half the world still lives with inadequate financial recourses. The World Bank estimates that 55.6 percent of the world's population lives on less than two U.S. dollars a day.[1]

There are many factors that cause or aggravate poverty. Yet as you read in chapter four, the list of "usual suspects" that most people believe causes poverty may actually be more *symptoms* or *results* of poverty rather than the causes.

Poverty is complex. The causes and conditions are a tangled web of things such as corruption, exploitation, overpopulation, ignorance, injustice, ineffective economic systems, poor distribution, and many other factors. But most fundamentally, the problem of poverty is a spiritual problem. It isn't that impoverished people are poor because of their sin. Instead, the fact is that we live in a broken and sinful world in need of reconciliation and restoration.

Without this honest recognition of sin and its effects, attempts to alleviate poverty will be misguided. Think of the trillions of dollars spent in the last decades at home and abroad to help the poor. Has all that money solved the problem? We know it hasn't. Moreover, without the understanding of *who* and *Whose* they are, the poor will never understand their worth and God's intention for them and everyone to have enough.

*Future Impact* suggests that how one looks at the world (one's worldview) is a key to addressing the root causes of poverty and giving the poor a chance to make a difference in their own lives. Unbiblical worldviews are characterized by "hollow and deceptive philosophies" (Colossians 2:8); in other words, the lies which Satan wants to substitute for biblical truths. Being taken captive by such philosophies can lead to greed, hording, selfishness, pessimism, fatalism, hopelessness, and poverty.

We utilized the ideas of Darrow Miller extensively in our discussion of worldview in chapter four. Miller says, "A worldview is a set of assumptions held consciously or unconsciously in faith about the basic makeup of the world and how the world works."[2]

Since God has provided the essential building blocks for us to live with abundance, a key to true holistic child development is having and consistently living a biblical worldview.

## Three Basic Worldviews

As noted in *Future Impact,* Darrow Miller identifies three basic and broad categories of worldviews that encompass the worldviews of most of the people in the world. These are:

1. **Secularism.** Secularism is the worldview of most modern western societies. Secularists deny the existence of God and anything spiritual. They believe that life is the result of the interactions of matter and energy, time, and chance. For secularists, matter, (or the material world) is the ultimate reality. Secularists do not believe in any universal truths or absolute morals.

2. **Animism.** A second major worldview is animism in all its various forms. It is the broad umbrella of beliefs of Hindus, Buddhists, and many other traditional peoples, especially in Africa and Asia. This view devalues the material world but fears and placates the unknowable and unpredictable unseen world. "Spirits animate everything, and everything moves toward oneness of spirit. The

real world is unseen, truth is hidden and irrational, all is mystery . . . filled with evil . . . [and] amoral."

**3. Theism.** Theism is Miller's term for a biblical worldview. God exists and is personal and rational. He created a universe of physical and spiritual dimensions. Truth, as revealed by God, can be known by man. God's character establishes absolute morals. All Bible-believing Christians should hold to some form of this worldview.

What difference does a worldview make? To begin, animists and secularists say there is no absolute truth, or at least that truth is unknowable. That often leads to treating life as though there are no standards for morality, knowledge, relationships, or anything else. A biblical worldview says we can know truth both in principle and in the Person of Jesus Christ.

Animists and secularists tend to believe that nature has dominion over mankind, not the other way around. Animists believe we are at the mercy of the alignment of the stars, planets, or unpredictable natural forces, which cannot be understood, but often must be appeased. Once in the course of three or four days on a trip to Nepal, the traffic was repeatedly stopped for massive wedding processions. I finally asked, "Why are there so many weddings going on?" I was told that the dates were very auspicious, because the stars or planets were lined up in a certain way. These people didn't know that they have dominion over creation. They think that the stars and planets have dominion over them!

Most secularists believe that global resources are fixed and rapidly running out. Once they are gone, they are gone. But that may be only partly true. For millennia man's primary sources of energy were primarily burning wood and coal and the like. Then *using the mind God has given us*, we figured out how to use all that sticky black stuff in the ground, which before had been simply a nuisance or a curiosity, to power engines and all manner of machinery.

Will the oil eventually run out? Perhaps. But there is no doubt that *using the mind God has given us* mankind will discover other forms of energy. (Hint: Ever heard of a hydrogen bomb? There is a lot of energy in hydrogen, and hydrogen is the most common element in the universe. Imagine that one day transportation might be virtually free, just as communication has become today. It could happen.) The point is, resources are as much in the *mind* God has given us, as in the physical resources He has provided. The Bible says that God has give mankind dominion over *all* of creation. We are to use our mind to develop and adapt what we find in creation and steward and use it for our benefit.

One more point. Will the poor still suffer because of exploitation, corruption, and other aspects of the sinfulness of man? Of course. That is part of the larger reality of the results of the fall. But in knowing *who* they are, and *Whose* they are, at least the poor have better opportunities to overcome the debilitating aspects of pauperism and fatalism.

## INSIGHT

Note carefully, though, that *dominion over nature* does not mean abuse of nature. In fact, God has charged us to be stewards of His handiwork; to care for, protect, expand, and optimize what He has given us.

The idea that some people are born better than others also stems from unbiblical worldviews, especially stemming from animism. Many people believe that one's lot in this life is based upon one's performance or goodness in past lives. You *deserve* whatever your circumstances are in this life because of what you did or didn't do in your previous life or lives. This belief leads to fatalism and unwillingness to try to improve your life. Moreover, people—even children—needn't be or shouldn't be helped. The corollary is even worse—the way to a better situation in the next life is to *accept* your circumstances now. There is no need for self-improvement if you are in dire straits, either, because the way to better circumstances in the next life is to accept the difficulties of this life without complaint. What a powerful grip this lie of Satan has over people's lives.

## Reflection Questions

Satan recognizes the power of God's truth and at every point seeks to distort it. He wants us to exchange God's truths for lies (see Romans 1) or replace them with lies. For each of the following lies of Satan, what biblical truth can you state God wants children and youth to understand?

- You and I evolved from animals. God did not form or make us.

- The value of a child or person is determined by other people and society.

- The value of a person is based on their skin color, gender, skills, education, wealth, or appearance.

- A child does not have unique gifts, potential, and creativity from God to be developed.

- Boys are more valuable than and superior to girls.

- Children from some ethnic groups are born superior to others.

- God loves some people more than others.

What a contrast between this notion and the truth that we are all created in God's image! As God's children, we are given resources to help ourselves and others, including:[3]

- A mind—the ability to think God's thoughts after Him
- A heart—emotions, imagination, dreaming of new worlds, creativity, and art
- Personality—a temperament and one of a kind nature
- Dignity—made in the image of God
- A tongue—use our spoken words to create cultures that shape the world
- Tool making—to minimize drudgery
- A conscience—to distinguish right from wrong
- A will—to act and shape history
- A soul—to appreciate the nonmaterial world
- The potential for wisdom, the potential for self-constraint
- Technical knowledge and skills for music, sports, communication, languages, and the arts

In spite of the above marvelous blessings, which are part of being created in the very image of God, many people still choose to believe one of the most pernicious lies of Satan—that life has no purpose or meaning, and therefore no ultimate value. People either resign themselves to some cosmic "fate," or decide to eat, drink, and be merry without concern for consequences. Yet God desires that each of us have a future and a hope—building a life with meaning and purpose.

Human beings, including poor families and children, with God's blessing and guidance can be active and ambitious on their own behalf. Life does not have to contain the same hardships and limitations that it has had for generations. Poor families do not have to be complacent or fatalistic, accepting things the way things are. Poor children can hope for a better future. That is the work of holistic child development.

## Reflection Question

1. Discuss at least three examples of "hollow and deceptive" philosophies in the nonbiblical culture/society/worldview of which you are a part. How do (or might) these have a tendency to lead to poverty? How might they hinder the development of children and families in your culture or place of work? Contrast these philosophies with biblical understandings.

Think of the impact of one of the features of a secular worldview—like the "me first," "look out for No. 1," "you only go around once" mentality. Discuss how these may lead to greed and even oppression.

**APPLY IT**

Review chapter four again. Then interview the elders or pastors of your church to discover more about their perspective on the causes of poverty. How do they answer these questions?

- Why are people poor?
- What does the church do for the poor?
- What is the difference between a poor Christian and a poor non-Christian?

After you have discussed the above questions with your church leadership, you might wish to ask them the reflection questions that follow (or others in this Study Guide session). Then write two or three paragraphs that summarize their responses.

## Reflection Questions

1. Do you agree or disagree that a non-Christian worldview has a tendency to lead to poverty and destruction? Defend your position.

2. Show with examples from your own life/church/society how and/or why a biblical worldview will create tendencies toward wholeness and life.

# CALL TO ACTION

This week, what action step will you take to help others become more aware of the true cause(s) of poverty—and how worldviews make it better or worse? Perhaps this week you could take the time to discuss some specific secular values, such as individualism or "look after No. 1" with one or more teenagers in your life. Maybe you could speak up and help others understand how many of the things we often think are *causes* of poverty are actually *symptoms* or *results* of poverty? Or perhaps this would be a good time to reflect on other aspects of your own worldview and consider how it affects your outlook on poverty and children.

Whatever your response, write it below along with a deadline *within seven days* by when you will take action.

## Reading

*Discipling Nations* by Darrow Miller, 33-76

*The God of the Empty-Handed* by Jayakumar Christian, 44-74

*Truth and Transformation* by Vishal Mangalwadi

# SECTION TWO

# THE CHILD AND THECHURCH

# THE ROLE OF THE CHURCH

# THE ROLE OF
# THE CHURCH

## OBJECTIVE

Upon completing this session, the learner will be able to discuss some theological foundations from Scripture for holistic development and the Church's role in God's redemptive intent for all of creation.

CHAPTER FIVE

THE ROLE OF
THE CHURCH

For God did not send his Son into the world to condemn
the world, but to save the world through him.
John 3:17

The Bible tells us that God's intention is to love and redeem all of His creation. This is the central message of the entire Bible. Holistic child development is a theological response to the truth of a good but fallen creation, and of a God wanting to redeem not just individuals, but whole cultures and societies. God has used many people and instruments to further this intention—from creation itself, to the covenants He made with Adam, Noah, Abraham, Abraham's descendents, the nation of Israel, and ultimately through the sacrifice of His Son on the cross to redeem the whole world (the *cosmos*).

## READ

*Future Impact* chapter five, "The Role of the Church." Note the Bible passages and chapter content that will best help you address completing the above objective.

# THE NEED

The Bible records that God considered every aspect of his creation good. "And God saw that it was *good*" occurs several times as He formed the universe and its inhabitants. This repetition in the Scriptures demonstrates that He meant it. But there are still tendencies within and outside the Church to consider parts of creation—including children—as though they were anything *but* good. Sadly, when that happens, we also tend to minimize what God has commissioned us to do.

God has entrusted the Church with the responsibility to bless and redeem all of creation. In this session, we will look briefly at some of these theological insights—creation, the covenants, and Christ's redemptive work on the cross—in relation to holistic development, then we'll look more closely at the responsibility of the Church to carry out this intention.

## Reflection Questions

1. As you see it, what are the Church's three top priorities as mandated by God? Support your responses with Scripture.

2. How does your local church or fellowship demonstrate their responses to the priorities you listed?

As you read in *Future Impact*, chapter five is probably the most theological chapter in the book. It traces three theological themes in relation to holistic development. These themes are briefly summarized here. Scripture supports that in God's view, **creation is good**:

> God called the dry ground *land* and the gathered waters he called *seas. And God saw that it was good* (Genesis 1:10).
>
> The land produced vegetation: plants bearing seed according to their kinds and trees bearing fruit with seed in it according to their kinds. *And God saw that it was good* (Genesis 1:12).
>
> God made two great lights—the greater light to govern the day and the lesser light to govern the night. He also made the stars. God set them in the expanse of the sky to give light on the earth, to govern the day and the night, and to separate light from darkness. *And God saw that it was good* (Genesis 1:16-18).
>
> God made the wild animals according to their kinds, the livestock according to their kinds, and all the creatures that move along the ground according to their kinds. *And God saw that it was good* (Genesis 1:25).

## INSIGHT

John Stott writes that God's design in creating humans *for* community stems from His design for us as community-based beings: "These human but godlike creatures are not just souls (that we should be concerned exclusively for their eternal salvation), nor just bodies (that we should care only for their food, clothing, shelter, and health), nor just social beings (that we should become entirely preoccupied with their community problems). They are all three. A human being might be defined from a biblical perspective as 'a body-soul-in-community.' That is how God has made us."[1]

## Foundation Truths

Here are some key biblical implications of the goodness of creation on children's ministry, explained in greater depth in *Future Impact*:

- Creation is good though fallen (and worth redeeming): We must continue to invest in it to make it a better world for children.
- Creation has order: We can be optimistic about social change, which in turn can give hope for a better future for children.

## Reflection Questions

1. Do you think God looks on you, His creation, and considers you "good"?
   Explain your answer with biblical support.

2. In your own words, describe what implications do the truths about the goodness of creation have for children's ministries?

- Humankind (including children) has a special place in creation.
- Children are good, though they have a fallen nature. We need to empower children to fulfill their divinely ordered role of creating cultures.

## The Covenants and Child Development

God's intention is that all of His creation should reflect His own goodness and glory. As the Psalmist of Psalm 19:1 wrote, "The heavens declare the glory of God and the firmament shows forth his handiwork." Even after the fall, God's intention is to protect and restore His creation, for the benefit of everything and everyone, including children. He first began to do this through His covenants. The first was with Noah after the flood. "Though speaking with Noah, God clearly made His covenant not only with Noah's descendents, but with all other surviving life, and with the earth."[2] Here is a part of that covenant as stated in Genesis 9:8-10:

> Then God said to Noah and to his sons with him: "I now establish my covenant with you and with your descendants after you and with every living creature that was with you—the birds, the livestock, and all the wild animals, all those that came out of the ark with you—every living creature on earth."

Later, God made a more extensive covenant with Abraham. As recorded in Genesis 12:2-3, God says not only that He would bless Abraham, but also that He would bless all the nations and peoples of the world through Abraham:

> I will make you into a great nation and I will bless you; I will make your name great, and you will be a blessing. I will bless those who bless you, and whoever curses you I will curse; and all peoples on earth will be blessed through you.

These remarkable promises and blessings are for all of God's people, *including* the children.

## Foundation Truths

This blessing of the nations is a central theme of all of the Bible. (The word *nations*, or in the Greek, *ethnos*, and their derivitives occurs more that 1,000 times in the Bible). Isaiah 55:3-5 notes that it was also God's intention that His chosen people Israel would be a blessing to the nations:

> Give ear and come to me; hear me, that your soul may live. I will make an everlasting covenant with you, my faithful love promised to David. See, I have made him a witness to the peoples, a leader and commander of the peoples. Surely you will summon nations you know not, and nations that do not know you will hasten to you, because of the LORD your God, the Holy One of Israel, for he has endowed you with splendor.

## Reconciliation through Jesus Christ

This quote from Albert Wolters, offers great insight into the redemptive work of Jesus Christ on the cross in reconciling creation and humankind to God the Creator:

> [T]heologians have sometimes spoken of salvation as re-creation—not to imply that God scraps his earlier creation and in Jesus Christ makes a new one, but rather to suggest that he hangs on to his fallen original creation and *salvages* it. He refuses to abandon the work of his hands—in fact he sacrifices his own Son to save his original project. Humankind, which has botched its original mandate and the whole creation along with it, is given another chance in Christ; . . . The original good creation is to be restored.[3]

## Reflection Question

1. Read John 3:16-17. As you see it, in what kinds of ministries should a church participate on behalf of children, given that the Greek word for *world* (cosmos) refers to *the whole of creation*?

What implications do the covenants have for holistic ministries to children? At least the following:

- God's intention to bless *all* the peoples and nations *includes* children.
- From the start of God's covenant with his chosen people, God expects that the children will be included so that they too will learn to fear the Lord.
- Scriptures show that children and youth were often included in celebrations and remembrances. There was a high level of confidence in their ability to understand and participate in the faith development of the community.

God's love for the *cosmos* (whole of creation—both social structures and individuals) in John 3:16-17 provides the biblical basis for believers to participate in holistic development. And God has entrusted to His Church the mystery of reconciling all of creation to Himself.

## Reflection Questions

1. Give some examples of how your church or ministry participates in the redemption of all creation.

2. Building on the examples you just listed, consider your church or ministry's resources—human, financial, material, environmental, and relational. By optimizing those resources, what are three ministry activities your church could engage in (or is already engaging in) on behalf of children that address the redemption of the whole of creation?

## Foundation Truths

The Church has often not fulfilled its mandate for holistic ministry, because of a debate about the role of the church in evangelism and social action. In chapter five, review Adeyemo's eight different possibilities for the relationship between evangelism and social action.

- Identify a position that you believe is most suitable to your theological convictions.
- What worldview assumptions do you think influence your position?
- List at least five Scripture verses that influence your position.
- Do any of these possible positions influence you to understand your ministry differently? If so, how?

# CALL TO ACTION

Relief, development, and child development ministries are responses to God's call to empower others to realize their full potential in Christ. There are also vital activities that can demonstrate Christian dedication to redeem the whole of creation. Pick one of the ministry activities you listed in the previous section that you think you could somehow develop in the context of your local church or fellowship. *This week*, see if two or three others agree with your idea and assessment.

## Reading

*Creation Regained* by Albert M. Wolters, 12-71

*If Jesus Were Mayor* by Bob Moffitt, 51 -97

"Children and the Kingdom of God" by Jessie Stevens, *Together*, July-Sept. 1985

"The Debate Begins" by Timothy Chester, *Awakening to a World of Need*, chapter 2

"Face to Face with Need" by Timothy Chester, *Awakening to a World of Need*, chapter 3

"Lausanne: Congress, Covenant, Movement" by Timothy Chester, *Awakening to a World of Need*, chapter 6

"Evangelism and Social Action," *Lausanne Occasional Papers* (No. 21), Grand Rapids Report

*Two Structures of God's Redemptive Mission* by Ralph Winter

# WHY CARE FOR CHILDREN IS THE *PARTICULAR* RESPONSIBILITY OF THE CHURCH

# WHY CARE FOR CHILDREN IS THE *PARTICULAR RESPONSIBILITY* OF THE CHURCH

## OBJECTIVE

Upon completing this session, the learner will be able to discuss and show from Scriptures why care for children is the *particular* responsibility of the Church.

## KEY VERSE

1 Kings 17:23-24: "Elijah picked up the child and carried him down from the room into the house. He gave him to his mother and said, 'Look, your son is alive!' Then the woman said to Elijah, 'Now I know that you are a man of God and that the word of the LORD from your mouth is the truth.'"

## READ

*Future Impact* chapter six, "Why Care for Children Is the Particular Responsibility of the Church." Consider the Scriptures and reasoning that most strongly make the point that the Church has the particular responsibility of care for children as you review the chapter.

## THE NEED

There are a variety of secular initiatives that both promote and practice care for children and the needy. Christians can and do learn a great deal from their understandings and interventions. Yet if the Church is God's instrument in redeeming all of His creation, and *only* Christians can in fact do *holistic* development, then we Christians have a *particular* responsibility to care holistically for children, both inside and outside of the church.

## Reflection Questions

1. What are some of the indicators that the Church worldwide is not doing as much as it could to care for children?

2. What are some of the indicators that the Church worldwide is responding to the responsibility to care for children?

Chapter six suggests four biblical perspectives as to why the Church—us Christians—have a particular responsibility to care for children:

1. **Because only the Church can respond to the needs of the _whole_ person.** Our secular child development friends may do a good job in responding to the physical and, to some extent, the social development needs of children. But it is only Christians who can help children grow in wisdom and in favor with God like Jesus did. Only Christians (the Church) can provide the training and nurture for children to grow to love and trust Jesus as their Savior, and understand that God is their friend.

2. **Because God hears the children crying (and we Christians must hear it too).** Reflect on the story of Hagar and Ishmael in Genesis 21, then respond to the reflection question that on the next page.

3. A third biblical rationale for a Christian holistic response to the needs of children is that we Christians know that **caring for children dispels disbelief.** The story of Elijah and the widow of Zarephath in 1 Kings 17 is clear about this. The widow questioned the intent of both God and Elijah when her son died. When God restores the widow's son to life, she understands that Elijah is truly

## Reflection Questions

1. How can your church help children grow in wisdom? In stature? In favor with God? In favor with man?

2. Why are children crying today? List at least five physical, emotional, and/or spiritual problems children face in your country.

a man of God who speaks the truth—and that God must deeply care for her because He completely healed her son. We Christians must not be manipulative—caring only in order to foster faith—but recognize the reality that, just as in Jesus' time, caring for others in His name helps people see and understand the love of Christ

**4. Because only the Church can "remove the curse."** Malachi 4:5, 6 says, "See, I will send you the prophet Elijah before that great and dreadful day of the LORD comes. He will turn the hearts of the fathers to their children, and the hearts of the children to their fathers; or else I will come and strike the land with a curse."

No combination of supplies or material aid can remove a curse. Secular organizations don't have room in their operative worldview for curses and blessings. Only the Church can respond to the problem of a curse and turn a curse into a blessing.

## Reflection Questions

1. Do you agree that parts of the land where you live have been stricken with a curse? Why or why not?

2. Reflect on Malachi 4:6. What are the "curses" that have afflicted children in your country today? What part can you and your church play to remove them?

Review the key points in chapter six that support each of these reasons, and then answer the next set of reflection questions.

## Reflection Questions

1. Which of the four biblical perspectives, in your opinion, is the strongest reason why caring for children is the particular responsibility of the Church? Explain your choice.

2. Which of the four perspectives, in your opinion, would be most persuasive to your local church or fellowship? Explain your choice.

3. Which of the four perspectives, in your opinion, would be most persuasive to convince someone outside the Church that caring for children is the particular responsibility of the Church? Again, explain your choice.

## Foundation Truths

The Christian understanding of *dignity* is another reason caring for children is the particular responsibility of the Church. Christians know of the dignity and true worth of all God's children.[1]

Dignity is an inherent quality given by God when He created us in His own image (Genesis 1:27; Psalm 8:3-6). Dignity transcends age, cultures, gender, economics, education, ethnic groups, physical or mental ability, fame, titles, and prestige.

Dignity is not dictated by anything external. It exists even in the midst of imperfection. David restored the dignity of Jonathan's son Mephibosheth (see 2 Samuel 9:3-8) who, as a physically handicapped adult, had forgotten *who* he was and *whose* he was.

We don't give children dignity—they already have it. We must respect it, preserve it, and sometimes restore it. Dignity can be restored by kindness, by love, by respect, by honor. A child's life can be launched with a single word of encouragement or act of kindness.

APPLY IT

Too often the Church feels that it simply does not have the resources to respond to the needs of the children in the midst. But I believe that God will do for the willing, resourceful church exactly what He did for Hagar. He will open the church's eyes to resources—to precisely the resources that are needed—that they didn't know existed. Often those resources are right under our noses!

The Apply It section in the last session asked you to consider the full range of resources available to your church or fellowship. Today, consider the full range of resources available to *you*. (Here, remember to consider your church or fellowship as one of those resources). How can you utilize the resources God has given you? It might help you to write your responses down in the categories of wisdom, stature, God's favor and man's favor. Do what you can to attach specific resources to specific ways you can help children develop.

# CALL TO ACTION

Choose *one* item from your responses for the Apply It section in this lesson to implement *in the next seven days*. It need not be a complicated activity. You might consider volunteering in a reading program. Perhaps you'd enjoy coaching a youth athletic team. Maybe it's time you stepped up to teach a children's Sunday school class or to simply donate to help support a child health or nutrition program.

## Reading

"The Children the Lord Has Given Me" by Roy Zuck, *Precious in His Sight*, 45-70

"Bringing up Children" by Roy Zuck, *Precious in His Sight*, 105-126

"God's Big Agenda" by Bob Moffitt, *If Jesus Were Mayor*, 51-74

"The Church and Today's World" by Bob Moffitt, *If Jesus Were Mayor*, 99-128

# THE CHILD IN THE CHURCH

# FAITH DEVELOPMENT IN CHILDREN

# FAITH DEVELOPMENT IN CHILDREN

## OBJECTIVE

Upon completing this session, the learner will be able to defend a position on the 4/14 Window and discuss some stages of faith development in children and essentials of spiritual training.

## KEY VERSE

Deuteronomy 6:6-9: "These commandments that I give you today are to be upon your hearts. Impress them on your children. Talk about them when you sit at home and when you walk along the road, when you lie down and when you get up. Tie them as symbols on your hands and bind them on your foreheads. Write them on the doorframes of your houses and on your gates."

## READ

***Future Impact* chapter seven,** "Faith Development in Children." Please mark and/or take notes on the issues of both faith development and children's receptivity to the good news.

## THE NEED

Most child development workers can describe the process of mental, social, or emotional development that we expect as children grow. However, child development is not holistic unless it addresses spiritual development as well. This is one important matter in the discussion of Christian holistic child development to which only the Church can respond.

## Foundation Truths

With nearly two-thirds of children around the world still waiting to know Jesus, it is not time to stop sharing the good news. However, we must continually examine *how* we do it. Sylvia Foth advises,[1]

**Learn, first, from the child.** Realize that the Jesus pointed to a child as the greatest example of a true kingdom citizen. Any child, even an unbeliever, can teach an observant adult about Jesus' kingdom priorities. What do you learn from a child about the kingdom of Christ? What do you learn about yourself? How are you convicted to grow and change to become more like a child?

**Treat children as people.** Children and youth need time to talk, to share, to process, to ask questions, to wonder, and even to decide later. Forgive my saying so, but sometimes children are treated almost like farm animals herded together for a corporate salvation prayer. Or they're treated like machines: Ask them to answer a rehearsed question, repeat a prayer, and the deed is done. Or they're treated with magical thinking: Give a Bible tract to a child who can't read, send him or her home, and hope a disciple magically appears overnight.

**Be aware of their journey.** Some of us remember a first, single point in time when we decided to follow Jesus. Some of us don't remember such a point in time. Children need reinforcement and encouragement as they take each important step to make Jesus their own Savior and Lord.

**Include the family.** God placed children in their families for a reason. We must honor the family God gave them.

What else might you include on your list of recommendations to those who want to reach children in today's world? With much prayer and humility, we press through these questions. Millions of children around the world are counting on us to figure it out.

## Reflection Question

1. Based on your reading and own experience, what are some sensitivities one should bring in sharing faith with an elementary-aged child? A secondary school-aged youth?

There is no need to wait until children are able to make complex decisions to introduce them to biblical truths. We do, however, have a responsibility to be both biblically sound and age-appropriate. How do we tell the good news of Christ in a way that is both understandable to a child at any age and biblically accurate? In chapter seven, we explored the age of accountability, the 4/14 Window and a staged approach of faith development to help sort through these issues.

## The Age of Accountability

Is there an age of accountability? The term refers to the time when individuals become mature enough to be morally responsible and consciously responsive to God's grace. The term is not found in the Bible but may be inferred from various Scriptures.

## Foundation Truths

Look at the following Scriptures. What do they say or what can you infer about an age of accountability from these Scriptures?

1 Corinthians 13:9-11: (Hint: Does Paul's analogy require that childhood and adulthood are different categories with differing capacities?)

John 9:20-21: "Ask him. He is of age; he will speak for himself."

Deuteronomy 1:39: "And the little ones that you said would be taken captive, your children who do not yet know good from bad—they will enter the land."

Jeremiah 1:6-7: "'Ah, Sovereign LORD,' I said, 'I do not know how to speak; I am only a child.' But the LORD said to me, 'Do not say, "I am only a child.", You must go to everyone I send you to and say whatever I command you.'"

## INSIGHT

Perhaps the closest thing we see in Scripture to a reference to an age of accountability may be in Deuteronomy 1: 37-40: "And the little ones that you said would be taken captive, your children who do not yet know good from bad—they will enter the land." This does not mean that these children were innocent, but their level of accountability was directly related to their moral awareness.

## Foundation Truths

Following is a checklist for spiritual training[2]—a set of targets at which to aim, prepared by Dr. James Dobson. The five Scriptural concepts should be consciously taught, providing the foundation on which all future doctrine and faith will rest. Dr. Dobson acknowledges that many of the items require maturity that children lack, and we should not try to make adult Christians out of our immature youngsters. However, I agree with him that we can gently urge them toward these goals during the impressionable years of childhood.

### Concept 1: "Love the Lord your God with all your heart and with all your soul and with all your strength" (Mark 12:30).

1. Is your child learning of the love of God through your love, tenderness, and mercy?
2. Is your child learning to talk about the Lord and to include Him in his plans?
3. Is he learning to turn to Jesus for help when frightened or anxious or lonely?
4. Is he learning to read the Bible?
5. Is he learning to pray?
6. Is he learning the meaning of faith and trust?
7. Is he learning the joy of the Christian way of life?
8. Is he learning the beauty of Jesus' birth and death?

## Concept 2: "Love your neighbor as yourself" (Mark 12:31).

1. Is your child learning to understand and empathize with the feelings of others?

2. Is he learning not to be selfish and demanding?

3. Is he learning to share?

4. Is he learning not to gossip or criticize others?

5. Is he learning to accept himself?

## Concept 3: "Teach me to do your will; for you are my God" (Psalm 143:10).

1. Is he learning to obey his parents as preparation for later obedience to God?

2. Is he learning to behave properly in church—God's house?

3. Is he learning a healthy appreciation for love and justice?

4. Is he learning that there are many forms of authority to which he must submit?

5. Is he learning the meaning of sin and its inevitable consequences?

## Concept 4: "Fear God. . . for this is the whole duty of man" (Ecclesiastes 12:13).

1. Is he learning to be truthful and honest?
2. Is he learning to keep the Sabbath day holy?
3. Is he learning the relative insignificance of materialism?
4. Is he learning the meaning of the Christian family?
5. Is he learning to follow the dictates of his own conscience?

## Concept 5: "But the fruit of the Spirit is . . . self-control" (Galatians 5:22-23).

1. Is he learning to give a portion of his allowance (and other money) to God?
2. Is he learning to control his impulses?
3. Is he learning to work and carry responsibility?
4. Is he learning the vast difference between self-worth and egotistical pride?
5. Is he learning to bow in reverence before the God of the universe?

In summary, a child's first few years should prepare him to say at the age of accountability, "Here I am, Lord, send me!"

## Reflection Questions

1. Do you believe there is an age of accountability?
   Explain your response.

2. Explain the age of accountability as though you were
   speaking to an 8-year-old.

## Stages of Faith

John Westerhoff III suggests four stages for the growth of faith in children.[3] The first faith stage in very young children is more experiential than understood. Children apprehend rather than comprehend. The hugs and affirmation they get from adults are, at least in part, credited to the God the adults worship. The absence of hugs and affirmation will mean that children will have a difficult time developing faith at all.

A second stage is affiliative in nature. Here, children and young people begin to identify with the faith of their parents or peers. It is important at this stage that the child senses that he/she is wanted, needed, accepted, and important in the church and faith community.

The third stage is characterized by questioning, doubt, and searching. Young people at this searching stage need to be allowed to explore and still be encouraged to remain in the faith community during their intellectual struggle and experimentation.

A fourth stage of faith development, according to Westerhoff, is owned faith. Due to the serious struggle with doubt that precedes it, owned faith often appears as a great illumination or enlightenment, but it can be witnessed in our actions and new needs. At this stage, people most want to put their faith into personal and social action, and they are willing and able to stand up for what they believe.

## INSIGHT

Parents and teachers can encourage and enhance owned faith by: [4]

- Connecting Scripture with everyday life
- Asking open-ended questions that demand mature thought
- Addressing a broad range of relevant and current topics
- Challenging those with owned faith to express their faith in practical ways daily
- Encouraging daily Bible reading and prayer
- Encouraging biblical action in response to social needs

## Reflection Questions

1. Write a few sentences where you have seen faith development illustrated in your life experience. You may address your own faith experience or your observation of someone else's faith experience.

2. Give an example from your culture or experience of the first faith experience of very young children being more "experienced than understood."

3. Give an example from your culture or experience of childhood faith being characterized by "questioning, doubt, searching and experimentation."

## The 4/14 Window of Receptivity[5]

Many think that it is practically impossible for a child under 12 or 13 years of age to have reached the mental, emotional, or spiritual maturity that is necessary for experiencing a genuine repentance for sin and submission to Christ as Savior. Yet a high percentage of people say that their own decisions to become a Christian were made before the age 14.

In survey after survey, in many countries and many cultures, in every case, 50 percent or more (sometimes much more) made their decision to follow Christ before the age of 14. It is clear that if children are going to make significant long-term life-changing decisions to follow Christ, those decisions will mostly be made before the age of 15. Or, to put it another way, there is a 4/14 Window of receptivity for children and young people to make a firm decision to follow Christ.

George Barna states, "If people do not embrace Jesus Christ as their Savior before they reach their teenage years, the chance of their doing so at all is slim."[6]

## Reflection Questions

1. Do you believe that there may be special receptivity for faith decisions amongst children between the ages of 4 and 14? Why or why not?

2. Did you embrace Christ as Savior during your 4/14 Window? What about the rest of your immediate family members?

APPLY IT

Survey at least 50 Christians—members of your church or other Christian groups—over the age of 30. Ask them at what age they made their first significant decision to follow Christ. Present your findings below:

| Between the ages of 4 and 14 | Number | Percentage |
|---|---|---|
| Between the ages of 15 and 20 | Number | Percentage |
| Between the ages of 21 and 30 | Number | Percentage |
| Over the age of 30 | Number | Percentage |
| TOTALS | | |

## CALL TO ACTION

This week, what action step will you take to help others become more aware of faith development in children? You could share the results of the survey in this session's Apply It. (There's every reason to believe your local church leadership would find this information very useful.) You could also share Westerhoff's stages of faith development with others and ask them if their faith journey followed the same steps. You might also discuss the Westerhoff stages with youth workers or teachers you know.

Whatever your response, write it down along with a deadline *within seven days* by when you will take action.


## Readings

*Transforming Children into Spiritual Champions* by George Barna, 28-76

"The Age of Accountability" by William Hendricks, *Children and Conversion*, 84-97

*Daddy, Are We There Yet?* by Sylvia Foth, 155-165

"The Child and the Church" by G.R. Beasley-Murray, *Children and Conversion*, 127-141

"The 4/14 Window: Child Ministries and Mission Strategies" by Dan Brewster in *Children in Crisis: A New Commitment*. Phyllis Kilbourne, ed., 125-139

# CHARACTERISTICS OF CHILD-FRIENDLY CHURCHES

# CHARACTERISTICS OF CHILD-FRIENDLY CHURCHES

## OBJECTIVE

Upon completing this session, the learner will be able to discuss and apply a wide range of elements that help make a church child-friendly.

## KEY VERSE

Zechariah 8:4-5: "This is what the Lord Almighty says: 'Once again men and women of ripe old age will sit in the streets of Jerusalem, each with cane in hand because of his age. The city streets will be filled with boys and girls playing there.'"

## READ

*Future Impact* chapter eight, "Characteristics of Child Friendly Churches." Note ideas that seem especially applicable to your church or ministry as well as the Scriptures you think support them.

# THE NEED

It is remarkable to enter a child-friendly church facility located in the heart of a rundown and sometimes violent neighborhood. The contrast can be startling, like walking from darkness into light. Where the streets outside are often littered with dangerous trash like broken glass and sharp-edged cans, inside the facility is clean and safe. Where the neighborhood outside is often filled with sounds of sorrow and profanity, inside the facility you hear the laughter and enthusiastic singing voices of children and staff.

We are to invite the children to come to Jesus, to learn, to grow, to serve, then to go make disciples. As adults become disciples, God then sends us out into the world to serve others and make new disciples, bringing them back into the Church. They, in turn, can become disciples and go out themselves. Thus the process is repeated and the church grows. This process is not only for adults, but applies to children and youth as well.

Children need a safe place for that process—a place that meets them at their point of development with what they need to take a step forward with Jesus. Jesus Himself said, "Let the children come to me—do not hinder them, for the kingdom of Heaven *belongs* to such as these" (Matthew 19:14, emphasis added). The children should be well-nurtured and cared for. There should be nothing about church programs and facilities, then, that hinder a child's safety and well-being nor their journey in faith.

## Foundation Truths

Keith White notes five essentials that must characterize a child-friendly church:

> **Security**—a place for relationship, exploration, play and development.
>
> **Significance**—to be assured as someone precious because of who they are; every child needs to know that there is at least one adult who is committed to him or her unconditionally.
>
> **Boundaries**—Boundaries are needed to feel safe, to develop, and to relate with others appropriately. We call these *rules, discipline* and *values*.
>
> **Community**—We are created for community and relationships. Are our churches providing that?
>
> **Creativity**—Children must be given opportunities to create, to make, and to shape.

## Reflection Questions

1. Think of one or two attitudes and actions that will encourage children in each of the five essentials.

   Do you consider the church in which you grew up to have been a child-friendly church?

2. If you didn't grow up in a church, would you consider the church nearest your childhood home to be child-friendly? Explain your response.

STUDY

There are numerous ways to make a church environment more child-friendly—in fact, too many to be covered here. When 8-year-old Johnny and Jennifer go into a church, what are some of the basic things they should receive or experience? *Future Impact* suggests several basic things that would seem important for all churches and for all children: You can no doubt add many items to this starter list.

## Basic Things that Children Should Get from the Church

What should a child expect from a church? The following:[1]

- Teaching of the Word of God. God demands from the Church that children grow up hearing and learning about the love of God for them and worshiping Him in a way compatible with their age and capability. This should be a priority in any church. Equipping in a church need not segregate the children from adults in terms of content, vision, and direction. In fact, it takes only a little creativity to plan a curriculum that is for the whole family. All that is needed is to custom design a common equipping track for adults, youth and children following the same theme, calendar, objectives, etc. Such a family-oriented approach naturally places the child in the midst of the church education program.

- Making disciples of children. Commensurate with age, each child shall be encouraged and given an opportunity not just to believe, but also to learn to follow Jesus through the teaching from the Word of God. This should be one of the key objectives of any church.

- Prayer. Children must be supported by the regular prayers of a church. The prayer items of the church should often include children's issues. Teachers should regularly pray by name for the children whom they teach. Further, the whole church should regularly pray for all of the children both corporately and individually. Parents should also be taught to pray for their children. And, of course, children themselves should pray regularly, giving thanks and seeking guidance and provision for their needs and well-being.

- Love and care. Children should grow and thrive in the love and care that a church affords them. A church should provide a listening ear to the children, and they should be free to share their views, needs, hurts, hopes, and dreams.

- Opportunities to participate in ministry. The church should enable children to serve in their homes, the church, and in their community. Children should be viewed as resources for ministry, and prepared for God's work by the church. The church should provide opportunity for children to find and express their spiritual gifts.

- A child-friendly church facility. The church facilities should be safe and attractive to children and childhood. There should be safe places for children to play

and be childlike—if possible, even with playgrounds or play areas.

- Appropriate classrooms. Each church should endeavor to provide attractive classrooms for children's Bible studies and other activities. Where possible, churches should provide child-size tables and chairs and colorful things on the walls at child-eye level (preferably things that the children themselves have produced).

- Qualified children teachers. Children's Bible teachers should get regular and continuous training so that they become and remain qualified. Teachers should be monitored to ensure that their teaching is sound and age-appropriate.

- Age-graded classes and curricula. The church should ensure that children receive regular, sound and biblical education based on children's age and capabilities.

- Family equipping and preparation. The church should educate and encourage parents to enable them to raise their children in accordance with the Word of God and in a way that protects children from harmful culture and other things that defile their consciences and their faith. When possible, the church should provide resource for the home (books, videos, tapes, etc.).

- Protection from harmful traditions. The church should make efforts to enable children to grow without being adversely affected by harmful traditional attitudes, beliefs, and practices.

## Reflection Questions

1. Of the items listed on the previous pages, which three do you believe are the most important to reach the children in your area? Why?

2. Of the items listed, which three would have been the most important to you as a child? Why?

## INSIGHT

Child sermons are often suggested as an addition to make a church's worship service more child-friendly. Child sermons can be an important way to include children and ensure that they hear a story or message in an understandable way. However, churches should think carefully about children's needs. There may be other better ways to include the children. Indeed, there are some good reasons not to do children's sermons.

The late James Montgomery Boice[2] said that children's sermons might distract people from the worship of God. They are meant to involve children in the worship service by offering something appropriate to their age. But the effect may be to focus the attention of the adults on the children rather than upon God.

Children's sermons may also contribute to "dumbing down" of the gospel message. As we have seen in lesson two, children have great capacity—far more than we often give them credit for—to understand the gospel message. "The goal for our children," says Boice, "should be to bring them up to the level of the adults—that is, to enable them to begin to function on an adult level in their relationships to God. But what we have succeeded in doing instead is to bring the adults down to the level of the children."[3] Boice continues:

> In many churches the sermon is hardly suited to any genuinely adult mind, the praise choruses would fit better at a high school rally than in the worship of the Bible's God, and the children's sermons probably speak as much to adult immaturity as to the children. In fact, the children's sermons are usually geared to the smallest children, and the older children are ignored.
>
> The defense of this bad practice is probably that children cannot follow what goes on in church. But that is not true. They can. And even if they cannot follow what goes on at first, our task is to teach them so they both can and will. And why not? It does not require much more time to teach children to participate in the worship service than it does to prepare some of the children's sermons I have heard.[4]

## Reflection Questions

1. Churches that are serious about ministering properly to children should weigh carefully the benefits and downsides of children's sermons. Based on Boice's insight along with your experience and reading to date, would you use children's sermons as a way to make a church more child-friendly? Explain your response.

2. Think about the idea of child-friendliness in churches. What other ways can you recommend to make a church more child-friendly? Pick three to five such items, list them, and provide a brief rationale for each one.

Here is a checklist on the child-friendliness of your local church.[5] After reviewing the checklist, you will be asked to do a careful rating of your church, then choose five areas for improvement which you will work on.

Arrange a meeting with a representative of your church. Have him or her help you choose five of the items to make priorities for improvement. Report back to your Christian education or child ministry leaders on your decisions.

| AIM 1: There is a vision for children's work | Yes | No | Unsure | Possible evidences |
|---|---|---|---|---|
| There is a common vision for children's work in the church. | | | | Vision Statement for Children's Ministry |
| Children's work is regularly on church leadership agendas. | | | | Minutes of meetings |
| We view children as real people, who have spiritual needs, and who have a role to play in our church . | | | | Interviews |
| **AIM 2: Training of workers and child protection is being implemented** | **Yes** | **No** | **Unsure** | **Possible evidences** |
| We recognize that we have a biblical responsibility to work with children. | | | | Interviews |
| Children's workers have been trained on how to teach children from a Christian perspective. | | | | Dated records of training |
| The church has an appropriate and monitored child protection policy. | | | | Child Protection Policy |
| All staff and volunteers in the church have signed a child protection declaration form. | | | | Child Protection Declaration Forms |
| All activities in the church are properly supervised and approved by the church leadership. | | | | Interviews |
| **AIM 3: The church building offers a safe environment.** | **Yes** | **No** | **Unsure** | **Possible evidences** |
| Group meeting areas are clean and safe. | | | | Tour of facilities |
| A first aid box is kept on church premises and can be accessed by all leaders. | | | | Location of first aid box |
| Details of emergency contacts are displayed where all people can see them. | | | | Location of notices |

| AIM 4: Nurture groups are available for children and young people. | Yes | No | Unsure | Possible evidences |
|---|---|---|---|---|
| The church provides age appropriate Sunday or mid week groups for young people and children. | | | | Church program |
| There are opportunities for children to seek God through the scriptures, teaching, and their personal experiences. | | | | Interviews |
| There is regular prayer with and for children and young people. | | | | Interviews |
| The church supports children with special needs. | | | | Tour of facilities; report of interventions |
| There is a realistic budget for children's work. | | | | Annual budgets or accounts |
| AIM 5: There are opportunities for children to engage in worship in the church. | Yes | No | Unsure | Possible evidences |
| Some services are designed to be for all ages. | | | | Service records |
| Services are planned in a way that children are appropriately engaged in spiritual development. | | | | Interviews |
| Children's leaders and children are involved in planning and leading child friendly services. | | | | Interviews |
| AIM 6: Suitable facilities for under 5s are available. | Yes | No | Unsure | Possible evidences |
| A special area is allocated for parents/carers to care for babies and very young children. | | | | Tour of facilities |
| Young children have access to engaging activities or appropriate toys and books. | | | | Tour of facilities |
| Christian parenting support is offered. | | | | Church programme |
| AIM 7: Children and young people are involved as equal members of the church community. | Yes | No | Unsure | Possible evidences |
| Children and young people listened to and consulted on church matters. | | | | Interviews |
| We include children in our attendance figures. | | | | Attendance lists |
| AIM 8: There are outreach opportunities. | Yes | No | Unsure | Possible evidences |
| The church's outreach programs include opportunities for children to participate. | | | | Interviews |
| The church is working with the local community officials to raise standards of child protection and awareness. | | | | Meeting records |
| The church helps prevent and delay problems through support of widows; heath care; parenting courses; feeding; family transition; income generating opportunities; etc. | | | | Annual report |
| The church continues to be involved in the child's life by promoting self sustainability for young people e.g. discipleship; vocational training; education; etc. | | | | Child records |

# CALL TO ACTION

This week, what action step will you take to help your local church or fellowship become more child-friendly? Will you begin to implement improvements on one of the five items you identified in the checklist? Will you talk about the importance of a child-friendly church to someone who has yet to be convinced that child-friendliness matters? Will you volunteer to be someone who helps children feel welcome in your church—perhaps even inviting a child to sit with you at the next service?

## Reading

"If I were a Child Today I'd Need . . . Developing Spiritual Kinship with Children," *It Takes a Church within a Village* by H. B. London Jr. and Neil B. Wiseman, chapter 4

"Family Traits of Child-Sensitive Churches Boys and Girls Loved Here," *It Takes a Church Within a Village* by H.B. London Jr. and Neil B. Wiseman, chapter 8

"39 Ways to Improve Our Impact on Children. You Can Make a Difference," *It Takes a Church within a Village* by H. B. London Jr. and Neil B. Wiseman, chapter 12

# CHILD PROTECTION IN CHURCH ENVIRONMENTS

# CHILD PROTECTION IN CHURCH ENVIRONMENTS

## OBJECTIVE

**Upon completing this session, the learner will be able to understand child protection issues in church environments, and develop and apply appropriate child protection measures in your own church or other care setting.**

## KEY VERSE

1 Corinthians 13:6, 7: "Love does not delight in evil but rejoices with the truth. It always protects, always trusts, always hopes, always perseveres."

## READ

*Future Impact* chapter nine, "Child Protection in Church Environments." As you review the material, be sure to somehow note specific points that might help you make your local church or child center safer for the children you serve.

# THE NEED

We dare not be naïve about the issue of sexual exploitation of children in organizations—including churches, which are in place to actually serve and protect children in every other way. Certainly, there are vastly more positive relationships and activities than the incidence of such shameful events. But they do happen. The issue is for us to make very sure that it doesn't happen to the children in our care.

We are opposed to all forms of child exploitation, including child labor, child prostitution, and all other forms of physical, emotional, and sexual abuse. As a fundamental commitment to the welfare of children, it is important that we be aware of, take a stand on, and take measures to ensure the protection of the children under our care that are supported by our ministries. All churches or organizations caring for children should develop training activities to ensure that all those in and around our program understand the critical nature of this problem and ways to prevent it. The emphasis here is on prevention of sexual abuse but the concern includes prevention of other kinds of abuse as well.

## Reflection Question

1. How would you respond to a church colleague who says, "We don't need those kinds of policies here. We are *called* to this work. No Christian would ever hurt a child"?

The focus here is on the components that make up an effective child protection policy that were offered in chapter nine.

## INSIGHT

For many generations, child abuse—particularly sexual abuse—was something too shameful to mention outside the church, much less among its members. But today in many countries, provinces, and states, child abuse must be reported to the civil authorities. Leaving such a known or suspected case of child abuse unreported often makes the child ministry or church involved with the child legally liable for harm to the child, *even if the ministry or church is not the source of the abuse.* That is why a child protection policy against abuse, and established procedures to report suspected abuse are essential.

## Nine Components of an Effective Child Protection Policy

As you review these components, think about which ones might have the greatest immediate impact on the safety of the children you serve. Also consider if there are components from this list missing in your church's child protection policy—and if the fact that they are missing leaves your church at risk.

### 1. Statement of commitment[1]

This statement summarizes why you have a policy and places it in the broader context. It should include:

- Definitions of child abuse
- An analysis of major child protection issues in your setting
- An analysis of the legal and cultural framework in your country

### 2. Communicating the commitment

A good child protection policy will clearly communicate the commitment to protection:

- Talking about child abuse and breaking the silence
- Awareness raising and training
- Including this policy in other staff/board manuals

### Foundation Truths

Child workers and ministry staff should be trained to recognize:

- Physical abuse
- Sexual abuse
- Emotional abuse
- Neglect
- Any other type of abuse common among children in your culture

## 3. Behavioral protocols

General guidelines for staff, volunteers, interns, visitors, donors, sponsors, guests, and partners include:

- Treating children with respect and dignity
- Description of appropriate behavior with children
- Two-adult-rule: One adult should not be alone—i.e., behind closed doors—with a child. If counseling or other confidential matters are to be discussed, it should be with a door open.
- Signed document saying the policy will be respected
- Action will be taken in cases of inappropriate behavior.
- Acknowledging that adults are responsible even if a child behaves in a "seductive" way
- Breaking these protocols will be grounds for discipline including dismissal.
- No hiring minors as house help

All visitors will:

- Be given a copy of the behavior protocols
- Be informed of the organization's commitment to protect children and know why it is an important issue
- Sign a written agreement to abide by these protocols
- Always be accompanied by project staff

## Foundation Truths

Basic principles for staff behavior guidelines are mostly common sense. They include:

- Avoid any inappropriate conduct.
- More than one adult be present at all times with children.
- Be careful of inappropriate emotional expressions from children.
- Consult a supervisor or seek professional counsel when in an uncomfortable situation with a minor.
- Use wisdom in handling children with emotional and psychological problems.

### 4. Child protection in our publicity and external communications

A good child protection policy will provide guidelines regarding the statements and images in our media and fundraising that we use to reflect our work with children.

- All communication should preserve the dignity and value of children.

- Pictures of children and stories should always be decent and respectful.
- Pictures should not imply relationships of power.
- Communications should be respectful of the right to privacy, not linking names with distinct locations and blurring or blocking the face of certain children at risk (e.g., a child in prostitution).
- Internet protocols, particularly related to sponsorship
- Behavior protocols for communications staff, which include explaining to children who you are, why you are asking questions and taking photos, what will happen to the photos, and obtaining permission from family/community leadership for use of images.
- Pseudonyms for children at risk

## 5. Ensuring all partners and stakeholders share the commitment

This component of the policy makes it clear that any project partners or other stakeholders must share our commitment to protect children. Anyone who may come into contact with the children needs to know about our commitment to child protection and share that commitment too.

## 6. Guidelines for screening and recruitment

A child protection policy will emphasize the importance of careful screening of potential candidates and recruiting procedures:

- Identifies procedures that reduce the risk of hiring someone who may abuse children
- Requires very intense attention to local law, so local lawyers need to be consulted
- This is for ALL staff, volunteers/interns, board members, and contractors
- A signed agreement for background check will be obtained during the recruitment process (where legally possible, a criminal record check related to abuses against children).

## 7. Responses to allegations

What procedure will be followed when allegations are made about possible abuse? The policy must detail the specific actions to be taken related to any allegations of abuse by staff/visitors (and others). It involves:

- Creating a culture that expects the reporting of suspicious behavior
- Treating both the victim and the alleged perpetrator with respect and dignity while an investigation takes place
- Believing the child until proved otherwise
- The development of reporting procedures
- A team approach (child protection worker, legal, personnel, management)
- Attention to confidentiality—(a need to know only basis)
- Written documentation of facts related to the investigation and outcome (confidential file)

## Reflection Question

1. Describe the screening procedures of adults, if any, that are used in your ministry setting to protect children.

- Following local laws as required and extra-territorial issues if a foreigner is involved
- Designating someone to deal with the media
- Including in the policy a statement allowing disclosure to future employers information related to the dismissal for suspected abuse
- Providing ongoing support to the child and offering support to the person accused

## 8. Advocacy and networking

Commitment to working with other groups interested in child protection to:

- Pray for wisdom and strength.
- Learn from other groups.
- Be involved in community, national and regional activities to lobby government, police, and others.
- Encourage and support training initiatives.
- Network with others.

## 9. Confidentiality

All applications, screening forms, reference forms, and any information obtained from use of these forms must be treated as strictly confidential. Adequate measures must be taken to ensure strict confidentiality.

**APPLY IT**

Think through the nine components of an effective child protection protocol in your ministry setting.

## Reflection Questions

1. Which of these are *most* effectively implemented and why?

2. Which of these are *least* effectively implemented and why?

3. List any improvements you and/or your church or ministry could implement within a few weeks that might strengthen your child protection protocol.

4. List any improvements you and/or your church ministry could implement over a longer period of time that might strengthen your child protection protocol.

# CALL TO ACTION

Because child protection is such a crucial issue, if your church or child ministry has no child protection policy, you might consider talking to the leadership there about drafting one. If that discussion takes place in the next week, you've done well!

Otherwise, *in the next seven days* do something that advances child protection in your church and/or to benefit the children in your life. Perhaps you could share the information about recognizing child abuse found in chapter nine. Maybe you could talk with the present staff of child workers and ask them how to improve child protection policies at your church or ministry. Record their answers, and report back to them and your child ministry leadership.

## Reading

"Guidance to Churches: Protecting Children and Appointing Children's Workers," *Churches Child Protection Advisory Service*, 1-22

"Protecting Children from Abuse" by Compassion International

"Spiritual Healing," by Dan Brewster in *Sexually Exploited Children*. Phyllis Kilbourne, ed., 144-160

# THE CHILD AND MISSION

# MISSION—WHAT THE CHURCH IS CALLED TO DO

# MISSION—WHAT THE CHURCH IS CALLED TO DO

## OBJECTIVE

Upon completing this lesson, the learner will be able to apply key concepts in the historical development and the current practice of missions to the ministry of holistic child development.

## KEY VERSE

2 Corinthians 5:18-19: "All this is from God, who reconciled us to himself through Christ and gave us the ministry of reconciliation: that God was reconciling the world to himself in Christ, not counting men's sins against them. And he has committed to us the message of reconciliation."

## READ

*Future Impact* chapter ten, "Mission—What the Church is Called to Do." A unique thing about *Future Impact* is the understanding that children and missions can be talked about in the same sentence. Until recently, if you were talking children, you weren't talking missions. And if you were talking missions, you probably weren't thinking children. That "omission" is now rapidly changing. Chapter ten begins to bring the two together.

## THE NEED

If Mission is at the heart of Church, have you ever thought that perhaps the main purpose of the Bible is to be a "Missionary Manual"? Perhaps the whole of the Bible ". . . is the story of God's Mission—why and how lost humanity must and will be redeemed by a loving God." [1]

As we look at the Bible in that light, we see that to redeem all people is the center of God's concern. And central to our purposes here, we may rest assured that "all people" includes children.

## INSIGHT

The word *nations* (or *peoples*, *languages*, or *tongues*) occurs more than 500 times in the Bible. Very often when we see those words, we can see some aspect of God's concern for or predictions about the fate of all the nations (or peoples) of the world. Consider these examples (emphasis added):

After this I looked and there before me was a great multitude that no one could count, from every nation, tribe, people and language, standing before the throne and in front of the Lamb. (Revelation 7:9)

May God be gracious to us and bless us and make his face shine upon us. That your ways may be known on earth, your salvation among all nations. May the <u>peoples</u> praise you, O God; may all the nations be glad and sing for joy, for you rule the <u>peoples</u> justly and guide the nations of the earth. May the peoples praise you, O God; may all the peoples praise you. (Psalm 67:1-5)

My name will be great among the nations, from the rising to the setting of the sun. In every place, incense and pure offerings will be brought to my name, because my name will be great among the nations, says the LORD Almighty. (Malachi 1:11)

He will rule from sea to sea and from the River to the ends of the earth. There desert tribes will bow before him. . . . All kings will bow down to him and all nations will serve him. . . . All nations will be blessed through him and they will call him blessed. . . . May the whole earth be filled with his glory. (Psalm 72:8-19)

Look at the nations and watch—and be utterly amazed. For I am going to do something in your days that you would not believe, even if you were told. (Habakkuk 1:5)

## Reflection Question

1. Do children figure into your church's thinking about missions? Explain.

## Foundation Truths

To introduce missions, **Future Impact** traces what some define as the three eras in the History of Modern Missions:

- The First Era (1792-1910)—founded by William Carey; missions to coastlands of Africa and Asia.
- The Second Era (1865-1874)—spearheaded by Hudson Taylor; missions into the interior of mission fields; formation of 40 interior mission agencies.
- The Third Era (1974-present)—inspired by Cameron Townsend; started Wycliffe Bible Translators; began to identify tribal and language groups and spawned a large group of specialized missions.

William Carey was a remarkable, holistic first-era missionary. Here is part of his story: **William Carey: "Attempt Great Things for God; Expect Great Things from God"**

William Carey was born in the United Kingdom in 1761. As a young adult he worked as a cobbler and pastor. In 1791 Carey wrote his famous treatise, "An Enquiry into the Obligations of Christians to use 'Means' for the Conversion of the Heathens."

The "means" Carey proposed were "sending mission" societies. In response, the Church Mission society was formed, and in 1792 they sent Carey himself to India as its first missionary. It was a five-month voyage. They never set foot in England again. During his 42 years in India, Carey buried two of his sons and two wives.

In August, 1800 Carey published the first of his Bible translations, a Bengali New Testament. In 1812 he lost years of work in a fire that destroyed whole manuscripts of translated material, many the only copies available. The fire, while a great tragedy, sparked worldwide interest in Carey's work and allowed him to raise money for many subsequent translations.

During Carey's years in India, he either translated himself, or supervised and corrected, 37 translations of the Bible. He also translated large numbers of Sanskrit and other Indian texts into English.

William Carey was also a holistic missionary, taking his gospel work into areas of helping children grow in wisdom, stature, favor with God, and favor with man. He started over 200 primary schools, including nearly 100 specifically for girls who were traditionally denied education. In 1818, he established the college at Serampore, which still stands, and today the Serampore group of seminaries are the only ones recognized by the government in India. Carey also advanced agriculture in India, and established many medical missions and health facilities.

Before Carey died at Serampore in 1834, he had earned the reputation among Indians as "The Father of the Indian Renaissance."

## Reflection Questions

1. Reflect on the holism of Carey's missions work. How might Carey's spiritual work have benefited from his involvement in education, medical care, and agriculture?

2. Missions today may be holistic but more specialized. How many specialized missions organizations and ministries are you familiar with?

## INSIGHT

### The One Child Policy—a Special Opportunity for Chinese Churches?[2]

China's One Child Policy is one of the ways that children are victimized. This policy has caused a disdain for girl children, and, neglect, abandonment, and even infanticide.

Unfortunately, when one seriously examines the one-child policy, it is clear that these are not the only catastrophes that have emerged. The One Child Policy means that children today have no brothers and sisters. But if the policy is continued for more than one generation, it also means that the child has no aunts or uncles, no cousins, no nephews, or nieces. In fact, the policy destroys the entire extended family, for such children have no relatives except their parents and living grandparents!

However, it may also be true that the One Child Policy in China may provide significant ministry opportunities for Chinese churches.

In urban cities or more developed places in China, even where conditional exemptions for going beyond the policy are available, many families do not opt for it because today's couples in China (and elsewhere) often prefer career success to children. These educated and economically better off couples are typically having either have one child or no children. Since the third generation is already being born under the shadow of this policy, a unique phenomenon has emerged that these little ones receive full attention of six adults—their parents and four grandparents. Together with the families' economic improvement, children are often spoiled by the material supply, but with a spiritual and social emptiness.

This opens the opportunity for local churches to reach out to these children. In demonstrating their love for the children, churches may be able to win the confidence of the parents and win their hearts for Christ.

In the countryside, the dynamic is quite different but still presents the chance to reach out for Jesus. In remote places where agriculture remains as the main economic activity and people are less educated, families often break the One Child Policy for various reasons, such as lack of knowledge on contraception or the traditional cultural preference for boys. Breaking the policy will cause suffering for both the "non-first" children and their parents.

The non-firstborn will not be entitled to any social benefits, such as free education. As the families are poor in general, these children will rarely have the chance to go to school and may suffer for lack of access to proper medical treatment. The parents and the children are viewed as outcasts.

But perhaps this too presents special opportunities for the churches. If the churches are willing to love these children by caring their practical needs, they will not merely minister to these needy children, but also have a good chance to reach out to their families.

A tragedy unfolding today, not just in China, but elsewhere, is that children are so devalued that they are not even born. Couples forego having children or abort those who are conceived. Make some statements about what that says about the value of children in those societies.

## Reflection Question

1. Read Malachi 2:15. Why did God create the institution of marriage? What does a one child policy, either official or *de facto,* do with that intention?

## Foundation Truths

Here are some important statements on mission by Andrew Kirk presented in chapter ten:

- Mission is the purposes and activities of God in and for the whole universe.
- The Church is missionary by definition.
- Mission is simply what the Christian community is sent to do.
- The main purpose of the Bible is that of a missionary manual.
- The whole of the Bible is the story of God's Mission—why and how lost humanity must and will be redeemed by a loving God.

Examine your church's missions program. See what kind of outreach is supported with your missions contributions. Look especially for places in your current missions program that impact children. Would you say that your church missions outreach thoughtfully addresses children? Is it holistic in nature, including ministry to the whole person?

# CALL TO ACTION

What action step will you take to help others become aware of how children have been, and are, a crucial focus of the Church's mission? One possibility is to help people whom you know connect the history of missions to current missions work involving children. Another option is to think through how a more holistic approach to ministry to children at your local church or fellowship could help create more disciples among those children and their families.

Whatever you choose to do, write it below along with a deadline *within seven days* by when you will take action.

## Reading

"The Bridges of God" by Donald McGavran, from "To Reach All Peoples," *Worldwide Perspectives*

"Today's Global Human Need" by Meg Crossman, *Our Globe and How to Reach It* (AD 2000 Series)

"God's Heart for the Nations" by Meg Crossman, from "To Reach All Peoples," *Worldwide Perspectives*

"Getting to the Core of the Core: The 10/40 Window" by Luis Bush, Evangelism and Missions Information Service

# PRACTICAL ISSUES IN MISSION AND CHILDREN

# PRACTICAL ISSUES IN MISSION AND CHILDREN

## OBJECTIVE

Upon completing this lesson, the learner will be able to discuss cautions in cross-cultural mission to children as well as strategies that advance the strategic value of children as mission resources and recipients.

## KEY VERSE

Luke 13:29-30: "People will come from east and west and north and south, and will take their places at the feast in the kingdom of God. Indeed there are those who are last who will be first, and first who will be last."

## READ

*Future Impact* chapter eleven, "Practical Issues in Mission and Children." Mark those points that have immediate impact on you, and will help you develop a strategic eye for children in mission.

## THE NEED

In chapter seven, we examined several matters pertaining to the faith development of children in largely Christian environments. Faith development was compared to the growth of a tree. We noted, however, that faith development for children in non-Christian environments would have very different dynamics. We now turn our attention more directly to issues pertaining to the child and Mission.

## Cross-Cultural Concerns in Mission, Children, and Family

The organization that I represent, Compassion International, includes Christian training as part of all the programs and projects it supports. We deliberately enroll children from non-Christian families. However, our expectation is that all our actions, intentions, and objectives and those of the churches with which we partner should always be transparent and obvious. We always make it explicit that Christian training will be provided to all enrolled children. We will never enroll a child, from any background, without the express consent of the parents or primary caregivers. Sometimes the consent is in writing, while other times, only verbal.

There are many instances in such programs where children give their hearts to Christ. Again, parents should always be made aware of what is happening. Parents of all children are encouraged to participate in Christian training themselves so that they know exactly what their children are learning.

However, more than just parental consent is needed before we would encourage our church partners to baptize new young believers. I support the position that persons under the age of 18 living in non-Christian contexts should not be baptized unless their parents are also prepared to be baptized along with them. The children then will have not just permission, but also the support and encouragement to learn what it means to follow Christ.

## Foundation Truths

Five cautions for cross-cultural child evangelism in sensitive situations:

1. Children should not be subjected to religious teaching and training without the knowledge and consent of the parents.
2. Christians should not pressure children for conversion in situations where the children and/or their parents are completely dependent on the financial and/or material support of Christians.
3. Christians should not seek the conversion of children with a patronizing attitude that distances oneself from their reality or suffering.
4. Christians should not offer a gospel that undermines, despises, or denies the validity of their culture.
5. Especially where a commitment to Christ may involve ostracism, rejection, persecution, or suffering, the consequences of a commitment to follow Christ must also be presented in a manner commensurate with the child's understanding and maturity level.

# Reflection Question

1. Reflect on the above five cautions of child evangelism in cross-cultural settings. Do you know of situations in which these cautions have been violated? Explain?

2. State at least two other cautions relating to the appropriateness or ethics of sharing your faith cross-culturally with children that may be necessary in your cultural context.

STUDY

## Foundation Truths

### The Significance of the 4/14 Window

We noted in chapter eight the "window of opportunity" for faith decisions between the ages of 4 and 14. We noted the extensive research that shows that most people who make a decision for Christ do so between the ages of 4 and 14, or, to use UNICEF's definition of childhood, before the age of 18. We called this the 4/14 Window.

The 4/14 Window is no longer just a catchy phrase, but an established fact. Consider this as well: Other research shows that up to 70 percent of people coming to Christ say that they were most significantly influenced by their peers or persons their age.[1] If these two statements are true, then children and youth are not only the most fruitful mission field, but also perhaps the most effective mission force.

- Where the churches are growing, most of the new converts are under the age of 18.
- Targeting the 4/14 Window results in strategic church growth and leadership development amongst children and youth. Indeed, the 4/14 Window is valid and so strategic, serious mission groups must give more attention to people in this age group.

## INSIGHT

### Children as Mission Resources

Sylvia Foth, in her excellent book on giving children a heart for missions called *Daddy, Are We There Yet?*, adds the following ideas for engaging and deploying children in missions:[2]

- Children can encourage others.
- Children can give and serve.
- Children can learn to share their faith.
- Children can go on missions trips. Many churches and families have brought children with them on their missions teams. Children learn to serve, to pray, to help. Take them into unreached areas, if you can. The experience can make a lasting difference in their lives.

## Giving Children a Missionary Worldview

I shall never forget the day I received a call from Dr. Gene Daniels. Dr. Daniels was doing research on people coming to Christ in India. In one area, he found that some 6,000 Banjaras, (an ethnic group in central India), had made decisions to follow Christ, and he began to investigate why that was happening. He called me thinking we would like to know that he had found that about 30 evangelists, mostly young people who had formerly been sponsored by Compassion, had been most influential in whole groups of Banjaras deciding to become

## Reflection Questions

1. List and discuss at least five reasons why ministry and mission to children and youth can be good mission strategy.

2. What are the implications of the 4/14 Window for your church, mission, or agency?

Christians. It seems that not only had we been helping some of India's neediest, but also helping to create a very effective force for missions once those children and youth were on their own.

Pete Hohmann talks about giving children a missionary worldview. The idea is to help children view the world around them through the lens of God's purpose. "We can give children no greater purpose," Hohmann writes, "that God's mandate to all believers: to make His name known in all the world. This is the purpose stated in Bible. This is the purpose we need to impart to our children."[3]

How might we impart a missionary world view to children? How can we communicate concepts about missions to children in a way that they can understand and see how they fit in? How can kids come to know they really can make a difference in God's global purposes? Hohmann suggests a number of ways. One possibility he recommends is teaching children the ten "P" words developed by Jan Bell of "Kids Can Make a Difference." The 10 "P" words are:[4]

- Purpose: God's purpose is to make His name known in all the world.
- Power: God makes His name known by demonstrating His power to people.
- People: God wants all people to know Him.
- People-Moving: People are moving all over the world, and this creates needs in their lives.
- Passport to the World: God has always told His people to go into the entire world, but we need to know what the world looks like.

- Preparation: Before we can go into the world, we need preparation.
- Possessions: Possessions are time, talent, money, and material things. We need to use them for God's Mission, not just for ourselves.
- Projects: We need to mobilize for action now.
- Partnership: We are in partnership with God in the task of making His name known in all the early
- Proclamation: Half the world still does not know about Jesus.

## INSIGHT

Our vision for children is often so future-oriented that we fail to see the tremendous spiritual capacity children have *today*. Pete Hohmann suggests that God has placed within children the same Holy Spirit that He has placed in adults, and He wants to powerfully touch and anoint kids.

## Reflection Question

1. Which three of the "P" words in the list would be the most effective in explaining missions to the children or youth you know? Why?

**APPLY IT**

Pick three to five "P" words from the list in the study section on the previous pages, and develop the concepts. What do they actually mean in your context? Provide some examples. Suggest ways to use them as the basis for a written strategy to encourage the children and youth in your church to engage in mission. Consider choosing words that you can turn into activities that will appeal to the children you plan to influence.

When you are finished, review your strategy with the leaders of your missions and children's ministries.

## Reflection Question

1. Discuss your experience of children and young people as *resources* for mission. How have you seen (or heard) of children being involved and making a contribution?

## CALL TO ACTION

This week, take one action step that will help others understand the vital role of children as both resources and recipients of mission. Your step could be taking the results of this week's Apply It section to discuss with a friend or a leader in your church. You could try out your "P" word strategy on one or more of the children or youth you know, or ask a young person to go through the "P" word list with you to discover which words are most compelling to him or her. Whatever you choose to do, write it down along with a deadline *within seven days* by which you will take action.

## Reading

"Conversion as Revolution" by Vishnal Mangalwadi in *The Quest for Freedom* and Dignity, chapter 6

Willowbank Report, Lausanne Committee for World Evangelization, 1974

"Children 'at Risk' Because They Have Not Heard the Good News: The 4/14 Window" by Daniel Brewster in *Celebrating Children*, 175-181

*Children: The Great Omission?* by Daniel Brewster and Patrick McDonald (booklet prepared for Lausanne III in Pattaya, Thailand, 2004)

*The Great Commissary Kids* by Peter Hohmann, 3-40

*The 4/14 Window,* by Luis Bush

There are other resources to teach children about missions. An excellent website with many resources listed is www.missionresources.com/teachkidsr.html.

# AVENUES FOR ADVOCACY

# SESSION TWELVE

# NONCONFRONTATIONAL
# ADVOCACY

# NONCONFRONTATIONAL ADVOCACY

## OBJECTIVE

Upon completing
this lesson,
the learner
will be able
to develop
appropriate
advocacy
strategies
for one's own
ministry setting.

## KEY VERSE

Proverbs 31:8-9: "Speak up for
those who cannot speak for
themselves, for the rights of all
who are destitute. Speak up and
judge fairly; defend the rights of
the poor and needy."

## READ
**Future Impact chapter twelve,
"Nonconfrontational Advocacy."**
Highlight those points in the chapter
that you think will help you develop
your thinking and action about
advocacy for children.

## THE NEED

Advocacy takes its roots from the legal profession. It means speaking or pleading on behalf of another. It has to do with speaking for, acting for, or defending someone or something before someone else who has the power to do something about the problem.

The Bible offers many examples of, and encouragement regarding, advocacy. Abraham is one such example:

> Then Abraham approached him and said: "Will you sweep away the righteous with the wicked? What if there are fifty righteous people in the city? Will you really sweep it away and not spare the place for the sake of the fifty righteous people in it? Far be it from you to do such a thing—to kill the righteous with the wicked, treating the righteous and the wicked alike. Far be it from you! Will not the Judge of all the earth do right?" The LORD said, "If I find fifty righteous people in the city of Sodom, I will spare the whole place for their sake." (Genesis 18:23-32)

The Bible promotes advocacy for children. Proverbs 31:8-9 states, "Speak up for those who cannot speak for themselves, for the rights of all who are destitute. Speak up and judge fairly; defend the rights of the poor and needy." Lamentations 2:19

says, "Arise, cry out in the night, as the watches of the night begin; pour out your heart like water in the presence of the Lord. Lift up your hands to him for the lives of your children, who faint from hunger at the head of every street."

In this session, we examine ways to be effective and biblical advocates for children.

## Reflection Questions

1. Besides Abraham and Moses, can you name at least two other advocates in the Bible?

2. Describe briefly how God's purposes were achieved through their roles in advocacy by making references to specific Bible verses, names, places etc.

Chapter twelve examined two basic types of advocacy. *Confrontational advocacy* often involves demonstrations, lobbying, marches, placards, and raising one's voice in public places. Sometimes it is more aggressive—like obstructing access or even through sabotage or other kinds of disruption. *Nonconfrontational advocacy* involves speaking out or enabling others to find their voices. Often it involves prayer, education, research, training, encouraging, networking, and other means of highlighting and addressing issues.

## Reflection Questions

1. As you see it, what are some advantages and disadvantages to confrontational advocacy? Nonconfrontational advocacy?

2. Do you see a place for confrontational advocacy on the part of the Church? Why or why not?

Advocacy can be a powerful tool for the Church. First, it is a mind-set that can influence all the ministries of the Church. Further, advocacy and development go together, especially when the avenues of nonconfrontational advocacy are implemented. As research, education, and training begin to impact children, advocacy can be a logical and effective forerunner for child development.

## INSIGHT

Advocacy and development go hand in hand. You have heard it said, "Give a man a fish, feed him for a day; teach a man to fish, feed him for a lifetime."

- But what if the fisherman has no access to the pond?
- What if the water has been polluted up stream?
- What if the wealthy landowner forces him to turn the fish over to him?

Often development doesn't get to the root of the problem. Advocacy often deals with the structural aspects of poverty, exploitation and injustice.

## Reflection Question

1. Give two examples where you have seen advocacy in action. Critique the effectiveness of advocacy in each example.

## What You Can Do as an Advocate

Here are a few things that every person can do to make advocacy a mind-set.[1]

- Be well informed about the situation of children in general and in your community in particular.
- Educate families, churches, and the community about different initiatives on behalf of children around the world.
- Lead a life at home, at church, and in your community that respects the worth of children.
- Pray about matters affecting children; be as specific as possible.
- Network with those who work for children and assist them in any way you can.
- Support the work of your church or other child-focused ministry, and encourage others to join in making the world a safer place for children.

## INSIGHT

Chapter twelve outlined six avenues for advocacy. They are:

- Prayer
- Vision casting
- Research
- Speaking out
- Networking
- Equipping/training

APPLY IT

## Foundational Truths

What is involved in advocacy?[2] Advocacy is:

- Asking why until you get to the root of the problem.
- Ensuring power is used well, enabling those without power to gain access to it, and helping those who feel powerless to see what power they already have.
- Education/empowerment of the powerless.
- Seeking justice for those who are oppressed or treated unfairly.
- Being a voice for the voiceless and enabling the voiceless to find their own voice.

Consider how the six avenues of advocacy from the Study section in this session may be implemented in your ministry setting in a nonconfrontational manner. With a friend, spouse, or church leader briefly discuss your approach of implementation and steps to avoid any potential risks, dangers, or hindrances. Give specific details, if possible.

## CALL TO ACTION

*In the next seven days,* how specifically might you make advocacy for children a mind-set in your church or organization? Or how will you make advocacy for children a mind-set for yourself? Review the "What You Can Do as an Advocate" list in this session for ideas. Whether you pick one of those items or come up with your own, implement it this week.

### Reading

*Compassion Child Advocacy Frequently Asked Questions,* Compassion International

*Advocacy Study Pack* by Andy Atkins and Graham Gordon, TEAR Fund, 1-43

# THE UNITED NATIONS CONVENTION ON THE RIGHTS OF THE CHILD

# THE UNITED NATIONS CONVENTION ON THE RIGHTS OF THE CHILD

## OBJECTIVE

Upon completing this lesson, the learner will be able to discuss the provisions and protections for children detailed in the Convention on the Rights of the Child (CRC), support or critique the problems that some Christians have with the CRC, and apply key portions from a Christian standpoint to one's own ministry to children.

## KEY VERSE

Proverbs 3:31: "Do not envy the oppressor, and choose none of his ways."

CHAPTER THIRTEEN

THE UNITED NATIONS CONVENTION ON THE RIGHTS OF THE CHILD

Do not envy the oppressor,
And choose none of his ways.
Proverbs 3:31

Christians and the Church are certainly not alone in their concern about the needs of children. Children also benefit from the activity of many secular NGOs, governments, and the United Nations. We turn our attention now to some of the major secular initiatives and documents promoting the welfare of children.

## READ

*Future Impact* chapter thirteen, "The United Nations Convention on the Rights of the Child." Note any part of this chapter that can help you fulfill the objective to the left.

# THE NEED

Caring for children is not limited to the Christians and the Church. Fortunately, many secular NGOs, governments, and the U.N. take action to benefit children. Chapter thirteen features a significant document promoting the welfare of children: the United Nations Convention on the Rights of the Child, or simply the CRC.

The CRC is the most respected statement regarding the protection and provision for children. It was ratified in the 1990s by all but two nations in the world—Somalia and the USA. Its origins go back to a visionary Christian named Eglantyne Jebb in the early 1900s. Early in 1920 Jebb oversaw the creation of the International Save the Children Union, which combined organizations from various countries working together to relieve child suffering in Europe.

The U.N. Convention on the Rights of the Child consists of three basic categories:

- Protection (protecting children from harm)
- Provision (providing what children need to live and develop)
- Participation (engaging children in their world)

In the Study section that follows, I will offer an unofficial summary of the key provisions of the CRC so you can determine its strengths and weaknesses from a biblical perspective.

## INSIGHT

Are rights central to a child's view of the world? Preliminary research indicates that relationships and play are more important to children. It would be as tragic as ironic if the move to attribute rights to them were to squeeze them further into adult moulds and institutions . . . Where is the balancing emphasis on their quality of life here and now? On play, on space, on daydreaming, on being as distinct from becoming?

The time is . . . overdue to remove our policies and services for children from the agendas of different government departments and to encourage a new way of thinking about childhood.[1]

## INSIGHT

Some major concerns about the CRC are:

- It gives away too many parental rights.
- It emphasizes rights that the child may not be mature enough to handle.
- It may make loving discipline, including spanking at home, a form of child abuse.
- Its position on rights may not be culturally appropriate.
- The idea of rights may be secular and not biblical.

## Unofficial Summary of CRC Key Provisions

### Preamble

The preamble reaffirms the fact that children, because of their vulnerability, need special care and protection. It places special emphasis on the primary caring and protective responsibility of the family. It reaffirms the need for legal and other protection of the child before and after birth, and affirms the importance of respect for the cultural values of the child's community.

### Article 1 Definition of a child

A child is recognized as a person under 18.

### Article 3 Best interests of the child

All actions concerning the child shall take full account of his or her best interests. The State shall provide the child with adequate care when parents, or others charged with that responsibility, fail to do so.

### Article 5 Parental guidance and the child's evolving capacities

The State must respect the rights and responsibilities of parents and the extended family to provide guidance for the child that is appropriate to her or his evolving capacities.

### Article 6 Survival and development

Every child has the inherent right to life, and the State has an obligation to ensure the child's survival and development.

### Article 7 Name and nationality

The child has the right to a name at birth, and the right to acquire a nationality and, as far as possible, to know and be cared for by his or her parents.

### Article 8 Preservation of identity

The State has an obligation to protect, and if necessary, re-establish basic aspects of the child's identity. This includes name, nationality, and family ties.

### Article 10 Family reunification

Children and their parents have the right to leave any country and to enter their own for purposes of reunion or the maintenance of the child-parent relationship.

### Article 12 The child's opinion

The child has the right to express his or her opinion freely and to have that opinion taken into account in any matter or procedure affecting the child.

### Article 13 Freedom of expression

The child has the right to express his or her views, obtain information, and make ideas or information known, regardless of frontiers.

### Article 14 Freedom of thought, conscience, and religion

The State shall respect the child's right to freedom of thought, conscience, and religion, subject to appropriate parental guidance.

### Article 15 Freedom of association

Children have a right to meet with others and to join or form associations.

### Article 16 Protection of privacy

Children have the right to protection from interference with privacy, family, home, and correspondence, and from libel or slander.

### Article 17 Access to appropriate information

Children have the right to access appropriate information . . . from a diversity of sources. The states shall encourage [dissemination of] information of . . . benefit to the child, and take steps to protect from harmful materials.

### Article 18 Parental responsibilities

Parents have joint primary responsibility for raising the child. The State shall provide appropriate assistance to parents in child-raising.

### Article 19 Protection from abuse and neglect

The State shall protect the child from all forms of maltreatment by parents or others responsible for the care of the child and establish appropriate social programs for the prevention of abuse and the treatment of victims.

### Article 20 Protection of a child without family

Provides for special protection for a child deprived of the family environment and ensures that appropriate alternative family care or institutional placement is available in such cases.

### Article 23 Disabled children

A disabled child has the right to special care, education, and training to help him or her enjoy a full and decent life in dignity and achieve the greatest degree of self-reliance and social integration possible.

### Article 24 Health and health services

The child has a right to the highest standard of health and medical care attainable, with special emphasis on primary and preventive health care, public health education, and reduction of infant mortality.

### Article 27 Standard of living

Every child has the right to a standard of living adequate for his or her physical, mental, spiritual, moral, and social development. Parents have the primary responsibility to ensure that the child has an adequate standard of living.

### Article 28 Education

The child has a right to free and compulsory primary education and different forms of secondary education. States should make higher education available to all on the basis of capacity.

## Article 29 Aims of education

Education shall aim at developing the child's personality, talents, and mental and physical abilities to the fullest extent. Education shall prepare the child for an active adult life in a free society and foster respect for the child's parents, his or her own cultural identity, language, and values, and for the cultural background and values of others.

## Article 31 Leisure, recreation, and cultural activities

The child has the right to leisure, play, and participation in cultural and artistic activities.

## Article 32 Child labor

The child has the right to be protected from work that threatens his or her health, education, or development. The State shall regulate working conditions.

## Article 33 Drug abuse

Children have the right to protection from the use of narcotic and psychotropic drugs and from being involved in their production or distribution.

## Article 34 Sexual exploitation

The State shall protect children from sexual exploitation and abuse, including prostitution and involvement in pornography.

## Article 35 Sale, trafficking, and abduction

It is the State's obligation to make every effort to prevent the sale, trafficking, and abduction of children.

## Article 37 Torture and deprivation of liberty

No child shall be subjected to torture, cruel treatment or punishment, unlawful arrest, or deprivation of liberty. Both capital punishment and life imprisonment without parole are prohibited for offenses committed by persons below 18 years.

## Article 38 Armed conflicts

Children under 15 years of age have no direct part in hostilities. No child below 15 shall be recruited into the armed forces.

## Article 39 Rehabilitative care

Child victims of armed conflicts, torture, neglect, maltreatment, or exploitation must receive appropriate treatment for recovery and social reintegration.

## Article 41 Respect for higher standards

Wherever standards set in applicable national and international law relevant to the rights of the child that are higher than those in this Convention, the higher standard shall always apply.

Pick three to five articles from the CRC summary that, in your opinion, most strongly support a biblical approach to child ministry and care. Show how they connect to your biblical understanding.

Pick three to five articles from the summary above that, in your opinion, could be construed as contrary to a biblical approach to child ministry and care, or which could easily be misused. Offer evidence that demonstrates how they might disconnect from Scriptural counsel. Are you aware of instances where this has taken place?

## Reflection Question

1. As you looked through the CRC article summary, did you find that you agreed with more of it, or less of it, than you thought before you began this session? Explain your response.

APPLY IT

Jesus gives us the *right* to be called children of God. Discuss how this biblical promise relates to the rights/promises detailed in the Conventional Rights of the Child (CRC).

Using your responses for this session's reflection questions—emphasizing those in the Study section—provide Scriptures that support or reinforce the provision or protection. Begin your own biblical "Rights of the Child" articles. There is plenty of material in *Future Impact* to help you along.

## Reflection Question

1. Review the concerns about the CRC noted in the text of chapter thirteen in *Future Impact*. How do they compare with the concerns you noted in the study section?

# CALL TO ACTION

This week, take one step that will expose someone else to the CRC and offer biblical affirmation or criticism of one or more of its articles. You might share your Articles for Biblical Child Ministry with someone. You could ask a friend or colleague to review the CRC summary with you. Perhaps one CRC article sparked an idea of how your church could improve its ministry to children, and you'll talk to someone who can take action on it.

## Reading

The Convention on the Rights of the Child. Unofficial Summary: http://www.crin.org/docs/resources/treaties/uncrc.htm.

"The 'Rights' of the Child and the Christian Response" by Paul Stephenson, *Celebrating Children*, 52-61

# NETWORKING ON BEHALF OF CHILDREN

# NETWORKING ON BEHALF OF CHILDREN

## OBJECTIVE

Upon completing this lesson, the learner will be able to discuss and defend at least five benefits of networking and apply networking principles to current ministries.

## KEY VERSE

Romans 12:5: "So we, being many, are one body in Christ, and individually members of one another."

## READ

**Future Impact chapter fourteen, "Networking on Behalf of Children."** Note the items that help you understand networking—and how it can benefit the children you serve—better.

## THE NEED

Networking helps develop our *proprioception*. Most people, without looking at their legs, will know whether they are crossed. The reason is that normal people have a kind of sixth sense called *proprioception*, which enables a person to sense the rest of the body. Paralyzed people often do not have this extra sense. The bedsores and other injuries they sometimes suffer are often due to an inability to sense their body and prevent injury.

In a sense, the networking of Christians caring for children helps us develop our proprioception. That is, it helps us *sense* the rest of the Body. When one part is hurting, other parts can respond. When one part is in need, another part can provide (1 Corinthians 12:12-31).

Experience has shown there are at least six benefits of networking, explained at some length in chapter fourteen. These include:

- Being effectively connected
- Maximizinh use of resources
- Improving development practice
- Developing professional standards
- Making quality training more accessible
- Providing better care for caregivers

## Reflection Question

1. Of the six benefits of networking listed on the previous page, which two do you believe to be the most important? Why?

STUDY

Please review **The Value of Networking** in its paragraph form in chapter fourteen, and in its outline form below.

## The Value of Networking[1]

### Networking shows appreciation.

1. Networking is a demonstration of unity in the body of Christ. (John 17:20-23)
2. Networking often reduces a spirit of competition and encourages a spirit of sharing. (1 Corinthians 1:12-13; Colossians 4:16)
3. Networking encourages accountability and understanding of the constraints to those who share the same vision understand the constraints. (Luke 19:12-27)

### Networking protects attitudes.

4. Networking encourages humility in larger organizations when they acknowledge that they do not have all the answers but can learn from others. (1 Corinthians 4:6-7, 18)
5. Networking helps smaller organizations to feel they are making a contribution beyond their own limited resources. (1 Corinthians 12:21-25)

## Networking improves effectiveness.

6. Networking recognizes that we live in a complicated world and that only by working together and sharing our combined God-given wisdom and resources will we accomplish the task. (Ecclesiastes 4:9-12)

7. Networking allows us to brainstorm together, share varying approaches, evaluate different strategies, learn from the mistakes and successes of others and provide some benchmarking for future activity. (Proverbs 13:10)

## Networking demonstrates fellowship.

8. Networking often encourages greater stewardship and efficiency by joining together to share facilities, reducing duplication, and limiting waste. (Titus 3:14)

9. Networking helps support and lift up those who are struggling in the task. (Isaiah 35:1-4)

10. Networking allows us to rejoice in success from wherever it originates. (Philippians 1:12-14)

## Reflection Questions

1. Which three of the Scriptures used in the above outline make the strongest arguments for networking, in your opinion?

2. Which category of principles above—shows appreciation, protects attitudes, improves effectiveness, or demonstrates fellowship—provides the best argument for networking, in your opinion? Explain your response.

## INSIGHT

Why network? Networking on behalf of children fills in crucial gaps from "the experience of others," as Patrick McDonald of Viva Network notes:

> Despite significant efforts to help "children at risk" at a grass roots level, the evangelical movement has a made a fairly marginal input into the areas of research and evaluation. Academically and technically, we live largely off the experience of others in our thinking about how to shape good childcare practice . . . Many . . . serious development and childcare organizations look upon the evangelical movement as energetic and compassionate while failing to take it into account as a serious entity. This has much to do with a low level of awareness of the actual nature and scope of our efforts, but I believe that it is also . . . a result of our failure to conduct serious research into practice, policy, and performance. One colleague described our efforts to help children as bearing much heat but shining little light.[2]

**APPLY IT**

Give at least one example of how you have seen networking improve your ministry (or how you think it *could* improve) your ministry under each of the six networking benefits listed in the Study section.

Then list potential networking partners—at least one per category—in the following categories:

- Local. For example, who would be a good local partner or ministry to help you with a special event for children, such as a vacation Bible school?

- Regional. Is there a church partner in your fellowship who could share insights with you regarding child ministry?

- National. Can a national organization or church association provide you with training or program ideas?

- International. What international organizations working on behalf of children could keep you current with best practices for child ministry or the latest in child research?

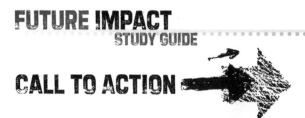

# CALL TO ACTION

What will you do to implement or share the value of networking on behalf of children? Perhaps you will follow through with contacting one or more of the networking partners you listed in the Apply It activity above. You could choose to discuss opportunities for networking with a potential local partner. You could visit the website of an international partner and gather information on recent child research.

Whatever you choose, set a deadline for action *within seven days*, and write down both the task and the deadline in this study guide or in your journal.

## Reading

*Reaching Children in Need* by Patrick McDonald, 71-117

Releasing children from poverty

# Compassion®
## in Jesus' name

## About Compassion International

Compassion International is a Christian holistic child-development ministry working to release over one million children from poverty. More than 50 years of child-development experience have shaped Compassion's understanding of children and childhood as critically important for individual, family, community and national transformation.

## The Compassion Difference

- **Christ Centered.** Each child has an opportunity to hear the gospel in an age-appropriate and culturally relevant way.
- **Child Focused.** Engaging each child as a complete person, we protect and nurture each child in all aspects of their growth.
- **Church Based.** We partner with local Christian churches to equip them for ministry with children.
- **Committed to Integrity.** We are dedicated to delivering excellent programs with complete integrity.

## Compassion's Mission Statement

In response to the Great Commission, Compassion International exists as an advocate for children, to release them from their spiritual, economic, social and physical poverty and enable them to become responsible and fulfilled Christian adults.

## Publishing at Compassion

God nurtures a very special relationship with the poor and the oppressed. Those without the power to change their lot. Nowhere do forces of poverty and oppression do more harm than in the lives of the world's poorest children.

That's why Compassion publishes books to help Christians understand the destruction poverty inflicts. To see the potential of children crushed in its grip. And to unleash the overwhelming power of the Church to free children—one by one, village by village, nation by nation.

When Christians spend themselves in the development of a child, they are invested in the purpose of God. These books inform that cause and inspire action. These books enable the Church to experience God's call of releasing children from poverty in Jesus' name.

## The Blue Corner

Every book that rolls off the press through Publishing at Compassion bears a symbol of God's intent. Our blue corner points back to Leviticus 23:22.

> When you reap the harvest of your land, don't reap the corners of your field or gather the gleanings. Leave them for the poor and the foreigners. (MSG)

This symbol is a reminder to leave a "corner of our lives" on behalf of the poor.

## SESSION 1: WHY CHILDREN?

1. Adapted from Wendy Strachen and Simon Hood, eds, "Evangelization of Children." *Lausanne Occasional Paper* 47 (2004), 12.
2. UNICEF, *State of the World's Children Report 2004.*
3. UNICEF, *State of the World's Children Report 2009.*
4. "Fullness of Life and Dignity of Children in the Midst of Globalization with a Focus on Street Children." Report of the Diakonia and Solidarity Team of World Council of Churches/Christian Conference of Asia Inter-Regional Consultation, Mumbai, India, 2004, 7.
5. Ibid., 7-14.
6. Wilson Grant, *The Caring Father* (Nashville: Broadman Press, 1983), 18.
7. Sylvia Hewlett, *When the Bough Breaks* (New York: Basic Books, 1991), 108.
8. Ibid., 79.
9. Ibid., 88.
10. Ibid., 107.

11. Linda Albert and Michael Popkin, *Quality Parenting* (New York: Random House, 1987), cited in Hewlett, 84.

12. Tom Hayes, *Jump Point: How Network Culture Is Revolutionizing Business* (New York: McGraw-Hill, 2008), Kindle Loc. 2531-37.

# SESSION 2: WHAT THE BIBLE SAYS ABOUT CHILDREN

1. Roy Zuck, *Precious in His Sight* (Grand Rapids, MI: Baker, 1996), 13.

2. Keith White, "A Little Child Shall Lead Them: Rediscovering Children at the Heart of Mission." Paper presented to the Cutting Edge conference, De Bron, Holland, 2001, 1.

3. Daniel Brewster and Patrick McDonald, *Children: The Great Omission?* Booklet prepared for Lausanne III in Pattaya, Thailand (Oxford: Viva Network, 2004).

# SESSION 3: THE MINISTRY OF CHILD DEVELOPMENT

1. John B. Wong, *Christian Wholism: Theological and Ethical Implications in the Postmodern World* (Lanham, MD: University Press of America, 2002), 14.

2. Marvin Olasky, *The Tragedy of American Compassion* (Washington D.C.: Regnery Gateway, 1992), 101-115.

Except for "Empowerment," all the subtitles from "Affiliation" to "God" were taken from Olasky.

3. "Empowerment" is used to replace Olasky's "Education" as the former gives a broader meaning.

4. Marvin Olasky, *Renewing American Compassion* (New York: The Free Press, 1996), 115.

# SESSION 4: A SPIRITUAL UNDERSTANDING OF POVERTY

1. *The Millennium Goals*, World Bank Development Indicators, 203, 5, www.worldbank.org.

2. Darrow Miller, *Discipling Nations: The Power of Truth to Transform Cultures* (Seattle, WA: YWAM Publishing, 1998), 38.

3. Adapted from Scott Allen and Darrow Miller, *The Forest in the Seed* (Phoenix, AZ: Disciple Nations Alliance, 2006), 44- 46.

# SESSION 5: THE ROLE OF THE CHURCH

1. John R.W. Stott, *Involvement: Being a Responsible Christian in a Non-Christian Society* (New York: Fleming H. Revell, 1985), 41.

2. Bob Moffit, *If Jesus Were Mayor* (Phoenix, AZ: Harvest Publishing, 2004), 55.

3. Albert Wolters and Michael Goheen, *Creation Regained* (Grand Rapids, MI: Eerdmans, 2005), 58.

# SESSION 6: WHY CARE FOR CHILDREN IS THE PARTICULAR RESPONSIBILITY OF THE CHURCH

1. My thanks to Dr. Wess Stafford for some of these thoughts concerning the dignity of the child.

# SESSION 7: FAITH DEVELOPMENT IN CHILDREN

1. Sylvia Foth, *Daddy, Are We There Yet?* (Mukilteo, WA: Kidzana, 2009) 160-161.
2. Abridged from James Dobson, "Dr. Dobson Answers Your Questions," in *Focus on the Family* 20(1):1966. Materials from the book *Dr. Dobson Answers Your Questions*.
3. Cited by Steve Wamberg, *Youth and Faith Development* (Prepared as a Continuing Education Training Module for Compassion International, January 2004), 6.
4. Ibid., 15.
5. Dan Brewster, The 4/14 Window: Child Ministries and Mission Strategies. *Children in Crisis: A New*

*Commitment,* ed. Phyllis Kilbourne (Monrovia, CA: MARC, 1996). This section on the "4/14 Window of Receptivity" is taken from a paper presented to the Lausanne Congress on World Evangelization in Pattaya, Thailand, October 2004 by Dan Brewster and Patrick McDonald called "Children: The Great Omission?" (Oxford: Viva Network, 2004).

6. George Barna, *Transforming Children into Spiritual Champions* (Ventura, CA: Regal, 2003), 34.

# SESSION 8: CHARACTERISTICS OF CHILD-FRIENDLY CHURCHES

1. Michael Shiferaw developed these points, which are an adaptation from *Covenant on Ministering to Children,* and unpublished document used to help African churches understand their responsibilities toward children.

2. James Montgomery Boice, "Children's Worship," *Christians Unite Articles,* http://articles. christiansunite.com/article2544.shtml.

3. Ibid.

4. Ibid.

5. Robert Choun and Michael Lawson, *The Complete Handbook for Children's Ministry* (Nashville: Thomas Nelson Publishers, 1993), 17, 18.

6. Michael Shiferaw, *Rate Your Church on Child Friendliness* (Unpublished paper).

7. H.B. London and N. Wiseman, *It Takes a Church Within a Village* (Nashville: Thomas Nelson, 1996), 211-230.

# SESSION 9: CHILD PROTECTION IN CHURCH ENVIRONMENTS

1. These nine child protection protocols are adapted from the presentation on the subject of Child Protection made by Dan Brewster and Heather McCloud at the Cutting Edge III, in Le Bron, Holland, March 2001.

# SESSION 10: MISSION--WHAT THE CHURCH IS CALLED TO DO

1. *World Mission: An Analysis of the World Christian Movement*, Jonathan Lewis, ed. (Pasadena, CA: William Carey Library, 1987), 2.
2. This case study is an adaptation of a portion of an article by Dan Brewster first printed in *China Source*.

# SESSION 11: PRACTICAL ISSUES IN MISSION AND CHILDREN

1. Laurence Singlehurst, *Sowing, Reaping, Keeping: People-Sensitive Evangelism*, 2nd ed. (Leicester, England: InterVarsity Press, 2006), 39.
2. Sylvia Foth, *Daddy, Are We There Yet?* (Mukilteo, WA: Kidzana Ministries, 2008), 204-205.
3. Peter Hohmann, *The Great Commissary Kids* (Springfield, MO: Boys and Girls Missionary Crusade, 1997), 21.
4. Ibid., 24, 25. Originally from Jan Bell, Kids Can Make a Difference. KidsCan@xc.org

# SESSION 12: NONCONFRONTATIONAL ADVOCACY

1. Adapted from *Compassion Child Advocacy Frequently Asked Questions* (Compassion International, 2004).
2. Graham Gordon, *Understanding Advocacy* (Teddington, UK: Tearfund, 2002), 30.

# SESSION 13: THE UNITED NATIONS CONVENTION ON THE RIGHTS OF THE CHILD

1. Keith White, "Small Matters," *Third Way Journal*, February 2002, 5.